D0213728

Praise for *Celebrity Diplomacy*

"While Thomas More and Benjamin Franklin achieved fame in fields other than statecraft, they did not set the precedent for Bono as a champion in the fight against global poverty or Angelina Jolie as an activist in defense of refugees. Andrew F. Cooper has performed a real service with his study of the application of star power to diplomacy and humanitarian causes, identifying both the benefits and the pitfalls of this thoroughly modern phenomenon."

Strobe Talbott
President, Brookings Institution

"The energy and influence celebrities can bring to global campaigns is of great potential. When done well, and with the appropriate sensitivities, including the recognition of celebrity power, their focused advocacy can complement the collective efforts of civil society as well as frontline development workers to improve the well being of the most vulnerable. In this study, Cooper shows how a select set of celebrities are using their star power to change the world."

Kumi Naidoo
Secretary-General, CIVICUS

"Bono and Bob Geldof have become principal voices in the fight against global poverty. The Gates Foundation is a leader in global public health delivery. Georges Soros is investing much more money in promoting democracy worldwide than many nation states. In *Celebrity Diplomacy*, Andrew F. Cooper charts out how an emerging transnational network of pop singers, business leaders, movie stars, and sport heroes is operating in global governance arenas and how influential it is proving to be. Taking into account 'celebrities as global governance actors' is something completely new in International Relations—a fascinating book."

Dirk Messner
Director, German Development Institute (DIE)

"Celebrity advocacy can no longer be ignored as a factor in global politics, although its impact in helping to address poverty in a sustainable manner is still to be determined. By recognizing the importance of this phenomenon, especially in the African context, Andrew F. Cooper takes an important step to deepening our understanding of a new feature of an old profession."

Elizabeth Sidiropoulos
National Director, South African Institute of International Affairs

---

"People invest their emotions in celebrities. Celebrity diplomats set out to re-channel those emotions toward issues, networking traditional politicians and giving them a share of their charismatic glow in exchange for their association. Cooper demonstrates the scope and intricacies of the networks involved. A pioneering work whose flow of presentation is as seemingly effortless as celebrity work at its best."

Iver B. Neumann
Author of *Harry Potter and International Relations*

"What a fantastic book! Well-written, thoughtful, and original—on a very hot topic that will make a great contribution."

John Orman
coauthor of *Celebrity Politics*

"A new type of transnational activist has emerged, both co-operating and competing with established diplomatic practitioners. Movie stars, musicians, and CEOs have grabbed new roles on the world stage, simultaneously levering their access to world leaders and mass audiences. The global system is increasingly open to and challenged by their participation in a manner that very few would have anticipated. Blending an appreciation of both complex forms of diplomacy and the exciting but unpredictable dynamics of popular culture, Andrew F. Cooper brings focus to this significant, yet under-analyzed, area of international relations."

Jorge Heine
Ambassador of Chile to India and
Vice President of the International Political Science Association

---

Celebrity Diplomacy

Andrew F. Cooper

Paradigm Publishers

Boulder • London

To my colleagues at CIGI, for expanding the horizons of innovation

green press
INITIATIVE

Paradigm Publishers is committed to preserving ancient forests and natural resources. We elected to print *Celebrity Diplomacy* on 30% post consumer recycled paper, processed chlorine free. As a result, for this printing, we have saved:

3 Trees (40' tall and 6-8" diameter)
1,239 Gallons of Wastewater
498 Kilowatt Hours of Electricity
137 Pounds of Solid Waste
268 Pounds of Greenhouse Gases

Paradigm Publishers made this paper choice because our printer, Thomson-Shore, Inc., is a member of Green Press Initiative, a nonprofit program dedicated to supporting authors, publishers, and suppliers in their efforts to reduce their use of fiber obtained from endangered forests.

For more information, visit www.greenpressinitiative.org

All rights reserved. No part of the publication may be transmitted or reproduced in any media or form, including electronic, mechanical, photocopy, recording, or informational storage and retrieval systems, without the express written consent of the publisher.

Copyright © 2008 Paradigm Publishers

Published in the United States by Paradigm Publishers, 3360 Mitchell Lane Suite E, Boulder, CO 80301 USA.

Paradigm Publishers is the trade name of Birkenkamp & Company, LLC, Dean Birkenkamp, President and Publisher.

Library of Congress Cataloging-in-Publication Data

Cooper, Andrew Fenton, 1950-
    Celebrity diplomacy / Andrew F. Cooper.
       p. cm. — (International studies intensives)
    Includes bibliographical references and index.
    ISBN-13: 978-1-59451-478-4 (hc)
    ISBN-13: 978-1-59451-479-1 (pbk)
    1. Diplomats.   2. Diplomacy—Social aspects.   3. Celebrities—Political activity.
    I. Title.
    JZ1442.C66 2008
    327.2092'2—dc22

                                                                        2007029913

Printed and bound in the United States of America on acid free paper that meets the standards of the American National Standard for Permanence of Paper for Printed Library Materials.

Designed and Typeset by Straight Creek Bookmakers.

11 10 09 08 07 1 2 3 4 5

Contents

Foreword

When I entered professional life, there was a marked distinction between diplomats and celebrities. One knew of diplomatic stars both past and of the moment. With very few exceptions, though, the most valuable work that diplomats contributed remained hidden from public view. Celebrities were another breed altogether. They could capture the public spotlight through their entertainment value. But one did not take them seriously or contemplate that the professional world of diplomacy would become intertwined with musicians, movie stars, athletes, and billionaires.

As this fascinating and important book by Andrew Cooper attests, that duality has broken down. Professional diplomats themselves can take on an aura of celebrity as their work is scrutinized in the public eye. Even more dramatically, these same diplomats—along with many politicians—are challenged by the concerted push by a high-profile cluster of celebrities into the international domain. Access to the highest level of decision makers is demanded and often obtained.

As I look back, I realize that this ascendant pattern should not have caught students of international relations completely off guard. Early pioneers such as Audrey Hepburn and Danny Kaye captured the imagination of some elements of the engaged publics in their creative endeavors for UNICEF decades ago. The full scope of this phenomenon, however, emerged after the end of the Cold War, with the massive surge of technical innovation and the expansion of space for nongovernmental organizations in the international arena.

What could not be anticipated were the sheer scale, intensity, and resilience of this phenomenon. Some celebrities participated in this activity as free-floaters, such as the late Princess Diana or Bono, whose advocacy work in support of increased funding for the Millennium Development Goals has had a surprisingly strong impact on many governments.

Philanthropists have also become much more visible players. Bill Gates, George Soros, and Ted Turner are breaking new ground not only because of the size of their financial contribution to international causes but also because of their personal involvement in global public policy debates. In particular, the Gates Foundation has become an uncontested leader in public health issues in developing countries, earning respect and admiration among the development community for the quality of its work.

Many celebrities, of course, have had formal affiliation with the UN through the goodwill ambassadors programs of many UN agencies. It needs to be acknowledged that in some cases this identification has not worked on a completely smooth basis. Not every goodwill ambassador had the aptitude of Audrey Hepburn. Learning from the experience gained over the years, UN agencies have developed stricter selection processes and strengthened their capacity to support and advise their goodwill ambassadors adequately.

Former UN secretary-general Kofi Annan was himself a strong promoter of celebrity involvement in the work of the UN. Working as his deputy for eight years, I witnessed his conviction that the UN can only gain from being better known and understood by the general public. He also knew that celebrities are sometimes better placed than politicians to convey important messages, that pop singers can preach AIDS prevention with young people in a way that no public official ever can. Annan created his own network of what he called "messengers of peace" and actively supported and encouraged the large number of celebrities acting on behalf of the various UN agencies.

Within days of my arrival at the UN Secretariat, I had the pleasure of hosting a lunch in honor of Luciano Pavarotti whom the secretary-general had just made a messenger of peace. In the following years, I saw every kind of celebrity—pop singers, business tycoons, movie stars, sport heroes—from all over the world beat a path to his office. A few were essentially motivated by self-interest but most were very sincere in their desire to "do some good for the world."

Neither the demands nor the actions of celebrities are going to save the world, but their engagement (and often their generosity) can help convince many in the younger generations that solutions to problems come in unpredictable but robust guises. Their activities also serve as a valuable signaling device that the status quo in terms of the global health/poverty/debt agenda remains contested by some who could easily enjoy rich, private, and even frivolous lives.

What leaps out from these pages of this book is the need to appreciate the emergent role of these celebrities in any comprehensive reading of global affairs in the new millennium. The image of celebrity diplomacy as a mere fad does not hold up. Cooper captures the essence of this vital and multidimensional phenomenon that will continue to grab our attention for years to come.

Mme. Louise Fréchette
Waterloo, Canada

Preface and Acknowledgments

My attraction to celebrity diplomats came about as part of a wider interest in new or complex diplomacy. Attention to a wide variety of topics has convinced me that the traditional modes of state-centric diplomacy face serious challenges, both in terms of normative claims of legitimacy and, with the compression of time and space, functional efficiency. Opportunities have emerged for an increasing number of nonstate actors to shape the agenda on a range of global issues. Familiar to many is the work of highly committed and creative nongovernmental organizations, yet underexamined is the role of very public individuals who are able to attract attention and mobilize resources to support their causes of interest.

This book highlights the role of personalities who ramp up the challenge to statecraft and its practitioners in a very different manner. A self-selected cast of celebrities—located in and around the worlds of entertainment and entrepreneurship—provides plenty of the ingredients that impart both a buzz and bite to their international activities. Their championing of global humanitarian issues, through a combination of idiosyncratic individual and sophisticated networked means, is exciting and often commendable. Yet it is also somewhat conceptually and procedurally bewildering. How seriously should celebrities be taken in world affairs? Should they and their proposals be given privileged access to world leaders and key international organizations? Can celebrities be diplomats in the way they talk and operate?

Thinking reflectively, albeit not uncritically, about the nature of this dynamic between celebrities and diplomacy is one thing. Producing a book that endeavors to tease out the various layers of this still evolving relationship is a different proposition altogether. My ability to do so in a relatively short time is a function of my debt to a multitalented cluster of people with whom I am fortunate to work and interact.

Being positioned at a new think tank has provided me with an enormously attractive and—as I reference in my dedication—innovative environment to do this type of research. The research agenda at the Centre for International Governance Innovation (CIGI) is aimed at achieving a better understanding of the ideas that will reshape and potentially help the world, as well as making those ideas accessible to diverse audiences. For facilitating such an environment in the case of the celebrity diplomacy project, I owe a great deal to John English, the executive director, and Daniel Schwanen, chief operating officer and director of research at CIGI. As with all my research activities, the project could not have been launched or completed without the vision of Jim Balsillie, chairman of the board of CIGI. His focused imagination and generosity matches those of any of the individuals examined in this book.

I am especially pleased that Madame Louise Fréchette, the first United Nations deputy secretary-general, and currently an esteemed colleague as a distinguished fellow at CIGI, has undertaken to write the Foreword to the book. That she did so is not only a personal honor to me but an indication of the significance of the topic.

I am also grateful for the encouragement I received from the University of Waterloo. President David Johnston, Vice President Academic and Provost Amit Chakma, and Dean of Arts Ken Coates have all been highly supportive, as have my colleagues in the Department of Political Science, including Richard Nutbrown and Gerry Boychuk. I have also benefited from the work of a number of excellent graduate researchers, including Asim Ali, Andrew Howard, Lloyd Pinsent, and Jennifer Jones.

Straddling the boundaries between my think tank and university commitments have been a number of other prominent researchers with whom I have interacted. They include Eric Helleiner, Jennifer Clapp, Patricia Goff, and Bessma Momani. All deserve recognition for lending their considerable expertise to refining this project.

Colleagues inside and outside CIGI with whom I have collaborated on a number of other projects have also provided their insights. The list of these individuals, although not exhaustive, encompasses Paul Heinbecker, Ramesh Thakur, Yoginder Alagh, Gordon Smith, Barry Carin, Maureen O'Neil, Rohinton Medhora, Andrés Rozental, Richard Higgott, Tony Payne, Tim Shaw, Colin Bradford, Thomas Fues, Dirk Messner, Elizabeth Sidiropoulos, Heribert Dieter, John Kirton, Helen Walsh, Madeline Koch, Annette Hester, Jean-Philippe Thérien, Nicola Phillips, Duncan Wood, and Daniel Drache.

Moreover, I have benefited from the detailed knowledge of an impressive network of specialized experts in reference to different aspects of diplomacy, most notably Jorge Heine, David Malone, Bill Maley, Brian Hocking, Bruce Gregory, and Daryl Copeland.

On a day-to-day basis, the entire staff of CIGI has been a joy to interact with. Dan Latendre, Will Hamilton, Neve Peric, Yvette Nanasi, Chris Mustakas, and the IGLOO team have been hyper-enthusiastic about this project from the beginning, as have Joy Roberts, Doug Roberts, Jennifer Jeffs, Alison DeMuy, Mohamed Hamoodi, and Agata Antkiewicz. The visuals associated with this project would not have been of the same standard without the efforts of David Yoon, Darcy Manderson, Darren

Cockburn, and, as an intern, Brian Peebles. And I have benefited enormously from the connections with the media possessed by Colleen Fitzgerald. Tamara Zur, Lena Yost, and Karen Daniel have all helped the project to run smoothly.

Kelly Jackson has been vital for both the intellectual shape and the delivery of this book. She not only did much to conceptualize the layout of the manuscript but did a number of edits that enormously improved its quality. Along with a number of other research activities devoted to complex diplomacy, she managed this project with efficiency and flair. She also helped to build an impressive team that includes Andrew Schrumm and Erica Dybenko. Andrew Schrumm significantly raised the level of the look in terms of both the completed manuscript and the Powerpoint presentation given on a wide number of occasions. He tracked down the photos and did much of the final inputting on the manuscript. Erica Dybenko copyedited and fact-checked with considerable efficiency, as did Ray Froklage at the last stages of the project.

As just noted, one of the main aims—and appeals—of this project has been to test the book via a number of public presentations. Of these, the most significant was my keynote presentation at the conference, CIGI'06. An added bonus was that my spouse, Sarah Maddocks, could attend this event and add her insights concerning the phenomenon of celebrity diplomacy. I can genuinely say that this is the book of mine that she has found the most interesting! My mother, Joan Cooper, and son, Charles Cooper, lent additional inspiration from afar.

The final thanks are for the professionals at or associated with Paradigm Publishers. Jennifer Knerr, Patricia Gimenez, and Melanie Stafford have efficiently run this project from the time we first talked about it, abetted by Mark Boyer and Steve Lamy. Professor John Orman of Fairfield University reviewed the book, and I thank him for his positive comments. I trust they are as pleased with the outcome as I am.

Andrew F. Cooper

Celebrity Diplomacy: Who Does It, How, and Why?

Celebrities have had a long association with the modern world of diplomacy. Benjamin Franklin—often considered the first American celebrity—assiduously worked the French Court of Louis XVI.[1] The quixotic reputation of Lawrence of Arabia remains indelibly connected to the Paris Peace Conference of 1919. And a stunning range of prominent actors, writers, poets, and entertainers—including Shirley Temple Black, Pablo Neruda, and Octavio Paz—represented their countries as ambassadors.

Yet, if not completely new, the enmeshment of late-twentieth-century and early-twenty-first-century celebrities in diplomacy is quite different in nature, scope, and intensity. The selection of Bono and Bill and Melinda Gates as *Time* magazine's 2005 persons of the year serves as just the most visible measure of how new types of celebrities performing an expanded range of activities are being recognized on the international stage.

Such a phenomenon cries out for some conceptual clarification as well as extended analytical treatment. Teasing out the motivations and modes of operation of this emergent cohort of diplomats is important, but so is the task of finding out exactly who these new celebrity diplomats are. Bono and the Gateses cover two very distinctive streams of activity that merit close attention. They do not, however, exhaust the list of celebrities who have ventured into the diplomatic world.

The personalities featured in this book perform their roles in global affairs through fundamentally different means than state officials and diplomats. The wave of celebrity entertainers and entrepreneurs is largely a public phenomenon, defined by an activism on the world stage that is cast as the stylistic opposite from the insulated and secretive world of mainstream diplomacy. An element of spectacle informs the activity. The mode of operation is decidedly populist in style. Few, if any, among these celebrities have any formal training, either academic or practical, in the workings of diplomacy. Their initiation is done without any extensive apprenticeship. The message they put out is cast in colloquial and sometimes markedly undiplomatic language. The site of diplomatic activity—if showcasing familiar diplomatic techniques such as communication and signaling—is decidedly unconventional. Instead of resident embassies and communiqués, their platforms of choice include interviews in a wide cross-section of new as well as old media and mass performances via staged events.

DO CELEBRITY DIPLOMATS DO DIPLOMACY?

If setting some parameters about who the celebrity diplomats are is important, an even more basic question must be teased out: Is what these entertainers and entrepreneurs do on the global stage actually diplomacy? Few of their activities mesh easily with the mode of behavior associated with traditional diplomatic culture. The biggest gap has to do with the criterion of representation, where there is no basis for seeing any of the celebrity diplomats as members of a formalized guild of diplomats.[2] Celebrities, unlike official diplomats, cannot easily claim that they speak for a constituency, whether defined as a cause or a people.

One way of getting around this issue of legitimacy is by taking a giant postmodern leap and simply adopting the view that everybody has the potential to be an authentic diplomat.[3] If diplomacy is wedded to everyday activity along a wide continuum and a robust and open-ended version of individual agency, the normative claims of traditional state-centric diplomacy are eroded.

If that is too big a stretch, a less diffuse argument can be made that some celebrities deserve to be included as diplomats on their own merit. For all their personal awkwardness—whether because of amateur enthusiasm or big egos—celebrity diplomats in clustered form do fit into some of the generic components of diplomatic culture. They combine the assertive individualism characteristic of the West with an appreciation of universal or cosmopolitan values. They abhor the use of violence. They engage in continuous dialogue, although not in a restrictive fashion, with multilateral forums such as the United Nations (UN) and the Group of Eight (G8). They are eager to balance what can be considered "megaphone diplomacy" with face-to-face engagement with official actors up to the level of chief executive, whether presidents or prime ministers.

The activities of celebrities on the global stage highlight as well the adaptive quality of diplomacy. Their enhanced role demonstrates the interplay between the domestic and the global in a very obvious fashion. Diplomacy has become porous not only in terms of formal structures but in terms of the fusion of informal elite dynamics. As celebrities push for recognition and support by becoming plugged into transnational policy making, the political elite use celebrities to boost their own credibility. This interplay is consolidated by the combination of publicity and symbolic and material resources that celebrities can generate.

The enhanced role taken on by celebrities reveals the cracks in the rigidities of the modern Westphalian state-centric system. Celebrity diplomacy emphasizes global reach in terms of problem solving, pushing for activity when and where it is needed. The Latin root of ambassador, *ambactiare* (meaning to go on a mission) has effectively become the mantra of diplomacy used by celebrities. All push hard against the constraints of the fixed way of doing things. All blend enthusiasm with outrage. All privilege a transnational trajectory over national sensibilities.

The current wave of celebrities squarely targets the arenas of global governance, global equity, and global regulatory issues. Efforts to end global poverty, to cancel debt, to expand programs of official development assistance, and to focus on HIV/AIDS and other pandemic health issues, all of which are heavily concentrated on Africa, would be on the top of most current lists of celebrity activism. The diplomatic project of Bono is at the core of this book, because of its blend of both representative and unique qualities. In the same manner as Nelson Mandela or Pope John Paul II, Bono's role transcends the boundaries of easy categorization. As the lead singer of U2 and cofounder of DATA (Debt, AIDS, Trade, Africa), Bono not only stands out as the archetypal celebrity diplomat but also bridges the gap between the Hollywood and corporate categories. In light of his pivotal role and reach in activities, it does not seem an exaggeration to talk about the possibility of the Bonoization of diplomacy.

Because of his imprint as a moral entrepreneur, Bono escapes most of the criticism for opportunism and superficial fluff heaped on other celebrities who have taken on a diplomatic profile. And this Teflon effect is well merited. A breathtaking gulf exists between Bono's serious and sustained enterprise and many other copycat celebrities who say that they "want to save the world." Bono comes closest to reproducing the operational brand of good international citizenship found in state and societal expressions of initiative-oriented diplomacy. But as we will see, Bono does not escape all criticism: a ripple of negativity has emerged, due in large part to the perception that his means have become distorted in the pursuit of his goals.

Getting the attention of elite decision makers is as salient as playing to a mass audience for Bob Geldof, who often is twinned with Bono in the hierarchy of celebrity diplomats. Geldof has embraced the role of maverick, cajoling and embarrassing state officials to do more in the priority areas he has targeted. What he does well is mobilize and shame. If Geldof has continued to stir things up, in the persona of "Saint Bob" or "Mr. Africa," he has also become part of the establishment. In this duality Geldof highlights an important contradiction in the mode of operations of celebrities. At least in posture, Geldof can be termed an extreme antidiplomat—impervious to the pull of socialization. But he has embraced and been embraced by the state elite. Geldof's extended process of estrangement has been not with the apex of power, but rather with sections of civil society in the global justice movement.[4]

Notwithstanding the projection of these two bigger-than-life personalities (and their ability to work as the smooth and rough edges in parallel forms of engagement), it would be misleading to elevate them to a position that completely disconnects them from other celebrities entering the world of diplomacy. In tune with the argument that the new aristocracy of stardom comes from a variety of sources, including "royal stars," "true" Hollywood stars, as well as musical stars, the candidate net for celebrity diplomats must be widened.[5] No discussion of this activity can leave out the legacy of the charismatic Diana, Princess of Wales, and the campaign to ban antipersonnel land mines, an initiative that also linked celebrity diplomacy and a hybrid form of state/nonstate diplomacy. Nor should the wealth of glamorous enthusiasts located in the world of Hollywood, whether pioneers such as Audrey Hepburn or the current wave with Angelina Jolie, Brad Pitt, Richard Gere, or George Clooney, be ignored. The mutual attraction of Hollywood and the UN is especially intriguing and deserves its own chapter before the analysis moves onto a detailed examination of the activities of Bono and Geldof.

SETTING SOME BOUNDARIES

Nuancing the nature of celebrity participation also helps set the boundaries about their relevance and performance as diplomats. A distinction needs to be made between the celebrities this book profiles as "celebrity diplomats" and those celebrities who have taken up political careers or causes exclusively at the domestic level. For the purposes of this study, the boundaries still remain tightly drawn in a number of important respects. One basic point of distinction is between official and unofficial roles. Once a celebrity runs for elected office, a line is crossed even if the same celebrity's diplomatic profile is expanded. Illustrations of this split abound in the United States from President Ronald Reagan to Jesse Ventura, a former professional wrestler turned governor of Minnesota, to Arnold Schwarzenegger, the "Terminator" who morphed into the governor of California.[6] But this phenomenon is global. Just one recent illustration is the experience of George Weah in Liberia. Weah, through his fame as the 1995 FIFA world player of the year and his leadership of the Liberian World Cup football/soccer team, had become a United Nations Children's Fund (UNICEF) goodwill ambassador with a high profile, especially among youth. Leveraging this opportunity, Weah used his sporting fame to mount a strong run at the presidency of Liberia in 2005.

The entertainers and entrepreneurs who have become ascendant diplomatic actors must be distinguished as well from the state officials and professional diplomats accorded celebrity status. This group deserves scrutiny in its own right. With greater space to operate, access to media, and in some cases, at least, an enhanced taste for self-promotion, some statesmen in this cluster both intersect and rival for attention of the type celebrity diplomats possess, as discussed in this book. It is true of extremely high-profile retired diplomats such as Henry Kissinger and Richard Holbrooke.[7] After all, Kissinger (under the moniker of Dr. K) tightened the connection between diplomacy and popular celebrity status. But it is also the case with the current superstar trio of ex-leaders, Jimmy Carter, Nelson Mandela, and, of course, the hyperactive Bill Clinton. All have, in one way or the other, an extended public life after political retirement as "wise men" and mediators.

For all their individualistic star power, diplomat celebrities remain embedded in the formalized system of state structures. Although occasionally taking on a freelance role, none can be entirely separated from the legacy of his or her official standing. Although now inflated with the potential to work on the global stage in some quite unfamiliar ways, the attention given to the initiatives taken on by ex-presidents and foreign ministers has some echoes of past experiences. A good number of notables from previous eras engaged in similar modes of innovative diplomatic practice. Herbert Hoover, for example, engaged in a number of high-profile activities in his postpresidential years, including a concerted effort to get food relief into Nazi-occupied Europe.

Thus, in contemporary circumstances, the distinction between performance of past or present official roles and elevation to the status of global icon has become blurred. Witness the hybrid role of Nelson Mandela, whose standing as a moral entrepreneur is at least as important as his position as a former president of South Africa. The significance of Pope John Paul II can only be understood by reference to his impressive ability to combine multiple roles: a religious leader, a diplomat whose impact stretched out over the ending of the Cold War, a promoter of dialogue with countries from Iran to Cuba, and an enormously popular celebrity.

It remains self-evident that official stature still matters. Kissinger wooed celebrity status for himself (and glamorous celebrities themselves) as a powerful insider within the administrations of President Richard Nixon and Gerald Ford. Mandela's superstardom cannot be divorced from his leadership of the African National Congress through the postapartheid transition in South Africa. Pope John Paul II had diplomatic standing as head of the Holy See, putting him in a very different class from other faith-based leaders. All could exploit a set of established links with the official diplomatic world unavailable to the new cohort of celebrity diplomats.

Other important distinctions can be made between celebrity diplomacy and alternative categories of advocacy via opinion leadership and charity work. A good deal of the activism by celebrities that can be categorized through these differentiated forms may spill over into the international arena. Oprah Winfrey is the classic celebrity opinion shaper whose work increasingly intrudes on the public global arena. Not only has she hosted the Nobel Peace Concert and promoted her innovative Oprah's Angel Network, she has become the conduit of choice by which celebrity diplomats reach a mass audience for their specific initiatives (whether the entry of George Clooney on the Darfur issue or Bono's Product Red campaign).[8] Nonetheless, not only does the good work she focuses on still rely on the support of a U.S.-based audience, the emphasis remains heavily weighted toward the personal as opposed to the public dimensions of self-improvement.

The same is true of the majority of Hollywood stars who have entered into the activist and philanthropic arenas. Ted Danson has campaigned for saving whales. Pamela Anderson has expressed outrage about the international seal hunt. Jessica Simpson has become the public face for Operation Smile, a nonprofit organization that provides reconstructive facial surgery to indigent children and young adults in the global South. As in the case of Oprah, much of this work is exceedingly generous in both donation and spirit, as illustrated by Sandra Bullock's contribution to the American Red Cross for the 2004

Indian Ocean tsunami relief efforts amid the declarations that "celebrity must count for something." Still, with some possible exceptions (Sting's Rainforest Foundation or Leonardo DiCaprio's association with the campaign against blood diamonds), initiatives of this sort must be distinguished from diplomatic activity.[9] To retain the label of "celebrity diplomats," individuals must not only possess ample communication skills, a sense of mission, and some global reach. They must enter into the official diplomatic world and operate through the matrix of complex relationships with state officials.

These distinctions fuel as many questions as they answer. Are celebrity diplomats via this definitional lens restricted to a small group of autonomous figures in the entertainment world entirely disengaged from societal connections? Whatever the impact of big personalities, it would be strange if their convictions emerged completely out of an isolated condition concerning what is going on around them. Moving from cause to effect, does freelancing capture the essence of their activities? Or is the individualism of this cohort complemented by the creation of various forms of organizational ties? And if organizational shapes take hold, what do they look like?

In some cases the push toward activism comes from a particular family background or set of influences. What complicates the issue of autonomy is when celebrities develop links with formalized institutional structures or societal actors. Princess Diana channeled her activities through nongovernmental organizations (NGOs), as has Richard Gere. Angelina Jolie may be moving in a similar direction. As in so many other ways, though, Bono shows the breadth of possibilities. After working initially through the Jubilee 2000 campaign, Bono moved to establish his own organization, DATA. Besides serving as a vehicle for Bono's increasingly ambitious project, this structure provides a hub by which other actors and activities can be connected via an innovative brand of networking.

The advantages of linking individual star power to a collective project are clear. Celebrities have the power to frame issues in a manner that attracts visibility and new channels of communication at the mass as well as the elite levels. As the head of policy at Oxfam argues: "What celebrities can do … is that they can help you reach an audience which you wouldn't otherwise get to, one which doesn't listen to institutions but responds to people."[10] Significantly, Oxfam has taken on its own celebrity spokespeople/endorsers, including Emma Thompson and Glenda Jackson in the UK. It has also endorsed a celebrity culture at other sites, including the World Social Forum (WSF).[11]

But NGOs have their own problems. They suffer from periodic bouts of performance fatigue. And they have come under some sustained critiques with respect to their own legitimacy and governance deficiencies.[12] Adding celebrities to the mix allows them to win renewed momentum for their campaigns. One payoff comes in the form of heightened leverage with state officials who want to identify with celebrities. Attention also allows for an acceleration of fund-raising activities.

The disadvantages of these links are as apparent. What happens when a celebrity loses his or her star power? Is there a risk that the cause will suffer a decline as well? Or, from a different angle, what happens when celebrities behave badly or in an opportunistic manner? In some cases—Geldof pops to mind on both categories—it doesn't seem to matter. His star power as a musical performer at the beginning of the twenty-first century is quite different from that in 1985! Yet, notwithstanding his faded credentials as a rock star, his celebrity power has continued to rise, albeit not without both private setbacks and public criticism.

Geldof stands out as an exception, though. In some cases—Michael Jackson serves as the most obvious example, as he was a prime organizer of the "We Are the World" all-star single—celebrities can become ridiculed for their causes as their careers go into a skid. In other cases, changes in personal circumstances can have a spillover effect beyond their private lives. A major Los Angeles fund-raiser for the NGO Adopt-a-Minefield had to be called off because of the divorce proceedings between its two major patrons, former Beatle Paul McCartney and Heather Mills. More serious still, celebrities sometimes cross another line, when their association with issues and ideas is so controversial that they are forced to remain freelancers. Jane Fonda has continued to be vilified as "Hanoi Jane." Sean Penn was widely viewed through a similar frame as an apologist for Saddam Hussein because of the vehemence of his antiwar activities (complete with an attention-grabbing trip to Baghdad in December 2002). Straining the envelope of cross-era analogies, Penn was compared to the main appeaser of the 1930s: "On the scale of historically maladroit gestures, Sean Penn's visit to Iraq evokes something more fatuous and vain even than Chamberlain's return from Munich."[13]

A narrow conception of celebrity diplomacy also ignores the fact that this core group may not be an all-encompassing listing. What about individual norm entrepreneurs outside the world of entertainment who have taken on some form of celebrity shine? This added element is exemplified by Nobel Prize winners beyond those connected with official diplomacy whether Nelson Mandela, Jimmy Carter, or Willy Brandt, the former chancellor of (West) Germany. Among transnational activists, Jody Williams from the anti–land mines campaign has gained some degree of celebrity allure.

Desmond Tutu, the former Anglican archbishop of Cape Town and chair of the South African Truth and Reconciliation Commission, has a recognized global sense of moral authority. And, if far more controversial in different ways, so does the Dalai Lama (in exile from Tibet) and Rigoberta Menchu Tum (the Guatemalan indigenous activist).

Beyond this group are those celebrity entrepreneurs who through the leverage of material resources have been able to propel themselves onto the global stage in the same trajectory as those situated in the world of entertainment. Ted Turner must be mentioned as one figure who has jumped out of this other incubator of nonofficial diplomats. And there are some other notables who straddle the worlds of entertainment and commerce, such as Sir Richard Branson (the chair of the Virgin Group of companies) as well as Richard Curtis (screenwriter/producer of *Four Weddings and a Funeral* and *Girl in the Café* fame).[14]

Still, center stage is given in this book to the activities of Bill Gates (chairman and former CEO and chief software architect of Microsoft) and George Soros (chair of both Soros Fund Management and the Open Society Institute). Not only do these two idiosyncratic figures possess tremendously deep pockets and a willingness to match material resources with voice, but just as crucially, they have utilized the World Economic Forum (WEF) at Davos in the Swiss Alps to project and amplify their activities. The unique blend of a concentrated theatrical process and the presence of big but diverse personalities resituates Davos as the core location for celebrity diplomacy. If the glamorous Hollywood types provide the buzz, Gates and Soros add some considerable bite on issues pertaining to the eradication of pandemic diseases and democracy promotion.

The focus on those two mega personalities leads in turn to the question of whether a built-in Anglo-sphere bias exists within the allocation of celebrity diplomat status. Even celebrities from non-English-speaking western countries seem to be neglected. Here the distinction between public intellectuals and celebrity diplomats provides a crucial hinge of distinction. Although numerous public intellectuals and pundits exist in countries such as France (as illustrated by the fame of Jean-Paul Sartre or Bernard-Henri Lévy), few span the boundaries between the two categories. One member of this small group is Bernard Kouchner, who combines a stature as a celebrity diplomat with a wealth of unofficial as well as official experience over his long and intriguing career extending back to his role as the cofounder of Médecins sans Frontières (MSF).[15]

The gap between the renown accorded to western celebrities, as opposed to individuals of a similar status in parts of the global South, must be considered as well. Nelson Mandela and the others mentioned above do not exhaust the limits of that category. South Asia provides a number of individuals who can claim to be celebrity diplomats; many of whom, although unknown in Hollywood and the West, have huge followings in the subcontinent. West Africa has produced a number of stars who have attempted to bridge not only the worlds of entertainment and societal activism but the religious divide between Christianity and Islam. Few of these celebrities, however, have been able to translate their local or regional fame into global celebrity status. Moreover, some of those who have the potential to do so fail, not only because of the structural obstacles imposed from the North (as seen most notably in the case of the 2005 Live 8 concerts), but also because of the temptations to enter the world of electoral politics (revealed to be a very attractive option for celebrities from the global South). George Weah provides just one illustration of this tendency.

REASONS FOR THE WAVE OF CELEBRITY DIPLOMATS

Just as important as questions of *who* and *how* is the debate about *why* celebrities have moved onto center stage in the diplomatic world as serious actors with some global reach. Through one lens, this phenomenon is taken to be part of a psychological/emotional development linked to celebrity culture in more generalized terms. Framed in this fashion, celebrities are taken to have some intrinsic attributes that provide them not only with status in their own realm of activity but credibility outside it. If celebrities can sell material goods as part of public relations or endorsement campaigns, can they not expand on their status and sell ideas and a sense of commitment on an issue-specific basis?

A second lens shifts the attention from the individual agent to the structure or environment in which celebrities operate. Globalization is privileged here, as is the transformation of information technology. Celebrity diplomats have hitched a ride on this technical revolution, or what Geldof terms "an electronic loop around the planet."[16] Cutting through the complications associated with negotiations and protocol, celebrities can connect immediately with a range of audiences. MTV and other mechanisms—including both text messaging and a proliferation of blogs about Bono and other celebrity diplomats—provide a multitude of connections to a global audience beyond the imagination a few decades ago. Select celebrities have a reach around the world far beyond what could have possibly been contemplated even at the time of a mega-event such as Live Aid in the mid-1980s.

A third lens places greater attention on the world—and contradictions—of diplomacy itself. The adaptive qualities of contemporary diplomacy and the connection between this recalibration in official statecraft and the turn toward celebrities have already been referred to. But the critiques of diplomacy have become far more extensive in the post–Cold War era.[17] In addition to the older brand of attacks (that diplomacy is inherently elitist and full of deceit) are newer claims that diplomacy has lost its relevance. To the question "Who are the diplomats now?" the possible current response is both everybody (NGOs, firms, citizen groups, and so on) and an increasingly narrow group of individuals (usually located in the central apparatus of government, via the White House, Prime Minister's Office, etc.).[18] Both trends open up huge opportunities for celebrities. If diplomacy is "everybody" and "everything," celebrities would appear to have a huge head start. They not only have the advantage of name recognition, but they can channel media focus onto their activities in a way that very few NGOs and firms can. If diplomacy is moving toward a concentrated state based on "big" men and women, why does this shift have to be located inside government circles? Why can't diplomacy be opened up to equivalent actors not fully embedded in the state? This expanded cohort would include celebrities intermingled with representatives from the business and NGO realms.

In either case celebrities can pick and choose tactics between the standard top-down repertoire favored by state officials—including personal and/or shuttle diplomacy—and a bottom-up approach associated with such initiatives as the anti–land mines and the International Criminal Court campaigns. Celebrities can act as creative hybrids, copying practices from other arenas while putting their own spin and media-savvy knowledge into the mix.

The mix of public diplomacy and advocacy through both official and unofficial mechanisms reinforces these advantages. At the cutting edge of the morphing of diplomacy in the twenty-first century is a greater emphasis on dialogue with diverse audiences through myriad channels. Yet, as in standard areas of diplomacy, most of the official mechanisms remain truncated by the need for protocols, etiquette, the subordination of delivery to process, a continued fight for resources, and claims of the national interest. Unofficial public diplomacy—epitomized by celebrity diplomacy—suffers from none of these deficiencies. Celebrities can be agile, contradictory, outrageous, and insulting. They also have an individual capacity to raise money and, in some cases, a store of backroom talent who can micromanage events and initiatives.

The final question pertains to the meaning of the overall phenomenon of celebrity diplomacy. Writing in the early 1970s, one student of international relations was expectant that a new sort of individual would play a part in the overturn of traditional diplomacy. Such a prediction was motivated in large part by features in the international system that would make it far more "hospitable to individual initiative," most notably technology that would act as a "booster-rocket for the individual."[19] The writer, whose mindset tuned into not only practical but also moral or normative claims, also asserted that the system would become far more responsive to individual needs by tapping into a "tradition of humanism, set against, and defying, the tradition of statism. It is flower power versus nation power."[20]

Has this prediction come true via Bono, Geldof, and others some forty years later? Some would argue, very strongly, yes! Others, it must be added, would demur or definitely say no! One criticism—voiced by other celebrities as well as noncelebrities—is that diplomacy (or politics for that matter) must remain a preserve of the specialist. Performers should entertain and leave it at that. The writer (and former Peace Corps volunteer) Paul Theroux for one has urged "white celebrities busy-bodying in Africa" to stay at home.[21] Eric Clapton for another has mused openly about the credibility of Bono and Geldof to perform a role beyond their professional competence. "They're only musicians," the former member of Cream and virtuoso guitarist pointedly said in one interview.[22]

Such sentiments tie back into two of the questions above. One is where participation in activities such as Live Aid or Live 8 crosses over into actions explicitly designed to have an impact on global affairs. The second is the question of where philanthropy ends and diplomacy starts. Although critical of political activity, Clapton himself has an impressive record of support for celebrity fund-raising. Clapton played at the first mega-charity concert, the 1971 Concert for Bangladesh. He also was one of the celebrity interviewees in a more recent documentary, *A Closer Walk*, about the global HIV/AIDS crisis.

FADDISH OR COUNTERPRODUCTIVE?

The notion that celebrity diplomacy is faddish activity that lacks credibility simply because of its source plays back into the standard realist concern that diplomacy should be done strictly by official diplomats. Gatekeeping, however, takes place not only through the actions of the long-standing guardians of the diplomatic craft but by the celebrity diplomats' own peers! It is all right for celebrities to raise money by playing at massive public events, but they should not stray beyond the line of either acting on or speaking directly to any diplomatic agenda. Kissinger and many others currently located in foreign ministries around the world would agree entirely with Clapton.

This criticism becomes more acrimonious when it takes on an ideological slant. In the United States, the main source of loathing with respect to celebrity culture comes from the right. Conservative authors such as James Hirsen are given extensive coverage on *The O'Reilly Factor* to magnify the theme of a radicalized Hollywood.[23] But this breed of attack dog has far less bite in terms of the diplomatic front than on domestic politics. The kind of commitment demonstrated by Angelina Jolie has made it far harder to attack her on her public life (although it is still open season on her private life). And the connection between the celebrities from the worlds of entertainment and business is puzzling to conservatives, as Bill O'Reilly acknowledges that Bill Gates can "walk the walk." Still, even if conservatives refrain from launching a full-scale offensive on celebrity diplomats, small-scale skirmishes continue.[24]

It is the radical left in the UK—albeit with celebrity champions of their own—that has sustained the strongest campaign against the intrusion of celebrities into global affairs. They view the celebrity diplomatic enterprise as a dangerous endeavor, for rerouting mass action on such issues as poverty and debt into the mainstream legitimizes the status quo. Bianca Jagger provides one well-known voice in this type of backlash against Bono and Geldof for their work on Live 8 and ONE: The Campaign to Make Poverty History, suggesting that cozying up to politicians leads to cooptation: "I know that we need to persuade politicians, but do we really need to sleep with the enemy? ... Although one cannot deny that Bono and Geldof have succeeded in bringing attention to Africa, one feels betrayed by their moral ambiguity and soundbite propaganda, which has obscured and watered down the real issues that are at stake in this debate."[25]

An offshoot of this left-wing criticism expresses frustration at the very attractiveness of celebrity diplomacy. In providing a new vehicle for a counter-consensus, it defuses, drains, or even suffocates more radical forms of protest and political mobilization. Because of its ability to act as a magnet for attention, any success of this form of celebrity activity comes at the expense of alternative voices, not only from the North (the antiglobalization or social justice movements) but also from the South. Collectively, celebrity diplomacy has subordinated other efforts such as the World Social Forum. Individually, it has enhanced the status of stars from the North over the fortunes of those potential celebrity diplomats from the South—a gulf highlighted by the marginalization of African performers, even at an African-centered event such as Live 8.

All of these levels of criticism can be embellished by a closer rendition of narratives across the range of individual celebrity diplomats. Yet amid all these significant and increasingly well-rehearsed flaws, celebrities add something to the world of diplomacy that deserves closer scrutiny. Just because it has evoked some elements of a backlash is not an excuse to dismiss this phenomenon as irrelevant or defective. On the contrary, controversy breeds considerable fascination with all the details of the phenomenon! Beyond these snapshots of who these celebrity diplomats are, there is a need to look more closely at their different categorizations and where, how, and why they have engaged in this activity. Only then can a more comprehensive depiction of this divergent wave of engagement with diplomacy be offered and the various criticisms leveled against this type of activity assessed.

"The Good Samaritans": Irish rocker Bono along with American über-philanthropists Bill and Melinda Gates were named *TIME* magazine's 2005 Persons of the Year (© 2005, *TIME* Inc.; reprinted with permission).

The growing cast of celebrity diplomats, if originating from a range of backgrounds and with differing levels of experience, certainly shares one trait: media savviness. Many in this group have parlayed their skills in public relations into full scale public awareness or lobbying campaigns.

The photos within this section demonstrate two prominent (yet intertwined) themes of this book: first, the ability of celebrities to play to the media, highlighting their aptitude to generate buzz; and second, their ease of access to world leaders and of mobilizing resources, demonstrating their diplomatic bite.

Audrey Hepburn in Somalia

UNICEF Goodwill Ambassador Audrey Hepburn holds a severely malnourished child outside a UN feeding center in Baidoa, Somalia, on September 24, 1992, only months before her death from cancer in January 1993. Shining the media spotlight on human suffering, she blended grace with an acute sense of discipline through her tireless UN work (UNICEF Photo HQ92-1179/Betty Press; reprinted with permission).

Danny Kaye in the Oval Office

UNICEF's first Goodwill Ambassador, Danny Kaye, developed the early model for celebrity advocacy. Here, he met with President John F. Kennedy in the Oval Office on November 28, 1962. Accompanying him that day were Judy Garland (in background), Richard Adler, and Carol Burnett (courtesy John F. Kennedy Presidential Library; reprinted with permission).

Princess Diana in Angola

Britain's Princess Diana traveled to Angola with the Red Cross in January 1997. As the most photographed person on the planet, she brought the media to the front lines in an effort to raise awareness of the devastating effects of landmines, particularly on children (AP Photo/Joao Silva; reprinted with permission).

Bono and Pope John Paul II

Bono met Pope John Paul II on the margins of Jubilee 2000, the debt cancellation campaign, on September 23, 1999. During their encounter, the two exchanged gifts: Bono received rosaries and the Pope accepted the musician's trademark sunglasses. Following their meeting Bono praised the pontiff, calling him "a great showman as well as a great holy man" (L'Osservatore Romano Photo/Arturo Mari; reprinted with permission).

Bob Geldof at Live Aid

Bob Geldof, chief architect of Live Aid, speaks at the start of African famine relief concert held at Wembley Stadium, London, on July 13, 1985. From this stage he made the famous cry, "Give us the fucking money!" The aggressive appeal was very successful, raising over $250 million, with an estimated 1.5 billion television viewers across 100 countries (AP Photo/Joe Schaber; reprinted with permission).

The Davos Supergroup

Networked celebrity diplomacy has evolved to a different stage. Here, the Davos super group poses during the G8 Africa plenary session at the World Economic Forum on January 27, 2005. With Bono are (left to right) former president Bill Clinton, Microsoft chair Bill Gates, South African president Thabo Mbeki, then-British prime minister Tony Blair, and then-Nigerian president Olusegun Obasanjo (AP Photo/Michel Euler; reprinted with permission).

Kofi Annan's Bilateral with Celebrities

On the margins of the 2005 G8 Summit in Gleneagles, Scotland, Bono and Geldof held a coveted bilateral meeting with then UN secretary-general Kofi Annan. The contrast in style between the two rockers is evident even in their posture, yet they often work in tandem; Bono as the charmer and Geldof as the provocateur (AP Photo/Alastair Grant; reprinted with permission).

Liberian president Ellen Johnson Sirleaf (center) welcomed outspoken billionaire philanthropist George Soros (left) and Queen Noor of Jordan (right) to a groundbreaking ceremony for a new school in an impoverished neighborhood of Monrovia on February 2, 2007. Soros's ability to mobilize resources is associated most with his Open Society Institute (AP Photo/Pewee Flomoku; reprinted with permission).

Famed Bollywood actor Amitabh Bachchan speaks at his invocation as UNICEF goodwill ambassador on April 14, 2005. Through this program, there has been successful celebrity outreach to the global South, where Bachchan has become a visible advocate for polio eradication and HIV/AIDS assistance (AP Photo/David Karp; reprinted with permission).

Senagalese singer Youssou N'Dour speaks during a media conference on the sidelines of the 2005 G8 Summit. Perhaps Africa's most recognized celebrity advocate for interreligious and intercivilizational dialogue, N'Dour was the only African performer invited to the Live8 main stage in London (AP Photo/Virginia Mayo; reprinted with permission).

Global Business Coalition AIDS Dinner

The 2005 Global Business Coalition (GBC) gala dinner brought together a cross-section of celebrity diplomats. From left, former U.S. diplomat and GBC president Richard Holbrooke, actress Angelina Jolie, Virginia chair Sir Richard Branson, and then-GBC director Trevor Neilson pose for the cameras in Washington on September 28, 2005 (AP Photo/Kevin Wolf; reprinted with permission).

Actors George Clooney (center) and Don Cheadle (right) met with outgoing secretary-general Kofi Annan upon their return from Africa on December 15, 2006. The two actors have used their star power to draw international attention to the ongoing humanitarian crisis in Darfur. Combined, they have produced documentaries and a book, made numerous media appearances, and lobbied world leaders (AP Photo/Frank Franklin II; reprinted with permission).

Product Red Campaign

For the U.S. launch of the Product Red line, Bono went on a televised shopping spree for the *Oprah Winfrey Show* along Chicago's Magnificent Mile on October 12, 2006. With Oprah's endorsement, Product Red gained instant credibility and name recognition in middle America (AP Photo/M. Spencer Green; reprinted with permission).

Comfortable both on the front lines and at the podium, actor Angelina Jolie was awarded the Global Humanitarian Action Award by the UN Association of the United States on October 11, 2005. In the tradition of Audrey Hepburn, she brings a capacity for compassion for the powerless with a global reach (AP Photo/John Smock; reprinted with permission).

CELEBRITY DIPLOMACY

Andrew F. Cooper

☆ 2 ☆

Star Power and the United Nations: From Audrey Hepburn to Angelina Jolie

The worlds of entertainment and the United Nations (UN) appear to be poles apart. The entertainment world is full of glamour, but it is also shallow and fickle. Celebrities are judged by very out-in-front and of-the-moment performances and appearances. There is space for new entrants to try to make it big. Yet the world of entertainment is also unforgiving in its judgment about who has reached and retained the top tier of celebrity status and who has either failed to do so or has lost that luster. Celebrities live in a here-and-now environment, with a huge incentive to lever their star power to full exposure in immediate fashion. Those at the top have considerable faculty to exploit their fame in either material or emotional ways. They have numerous requests to advertise and endorse products around the world. They also have the opportunity to brand or rebrand themselves, through an association with a host of causes or interest-based activities. The cult of the individual—in which a relatively few celebrities have huge name and activity recognition—is supreme.

The UN as displayed at its headquarters in New York is anything but glamorous. At the intergovernmental level, the only component of the UN on display is the General Assembly. And with very few exceptions (for instance, the dramatic appearance before the General Assembly of Palestine Liberation

Organization chairman Yasser Arafat in 1974, with his presentation of "an olive branch and a freedom fighter's gun"), this arena for all but the keenest aficionados is boring to the extreme. The work of the Security Council—particularly in moments of crisis such as the Cuban Missile Crisis or the run-up to the 2003 invasion of Iraq—is more exciting, with some permanent representatives making a name (and gaining face recognition) for themselves in the media. These moments, though, are rare and fleeting. The bulk of the work and decision making continues to be done by older men in suits in an environment largely concealed from view.[1] The UN continues to be rigidly hierarchical in form, a characteristic that has spilled over into its Secretariat and its field operations. Titles, as much as performance, are the measure of standing.

Amid all these differences, however, there is a synergy and sense of mutual admiration that belie an image of two worlds apart. Individual celebrities and the UN are not only attracted to each other but have built up a surprisingly close and extended web of relationships. Although not new, this connection became far more pronounced during the tenure of Secretary-General Kofi Annan, as a wider variety of celebrities was courted and became entangled in the UN system. Nor is this embrace of star power limited to a symbolic relationship in New York. The trend for celebrities to take on representational functions for specialized UN agencies and to work on their behalf, both at headquarters and in the field, has become ever more prominent.

To emphasize this connection is not to minimize the sense of awkwardness that continues to permeate the relationship between the two worlds. The UN has throughout its history flirted with celebrities when it wanted them to be the legitimizing faces of the institution. Most of the celebrities involved in this fashion have been little more than good-looking (sometimes extremely good-looking) adornments, adding increasing amounts of recognition and enthusiasm but little else. Whether by institutional design or through self-imposed limits, the celebrities kept within the restrictive boundaries of a tight script and mode of operation about what they could say and how they could act.

Those parameters are much harder to maintain in the twenty-first century. The celebrities most closely identified with the UN as early goodwill ambassadors conformed to a set model of behavior, but the more recent wave has stepped beyond these traditional limitations. The gulf in personality types can be gauged by the divergence between Audrey Hepburn and Angelina Jolie, positioned at the beginning and the end of this chapter, to demonstrate the move beyond a strictly conformist model of activity.

Both Audrey Hepburn and Angelina Jolie epitomize the mobilization of a glamorous enthusiast via the UN. What unites them is their mixture of commitment to a particular UN specialized agency and a capacity for compassion when confronted by disaster and human misery. Nonetheless, the stylistic differences between these two Oscar winners must be drawn out as well. Audrey Hepburn epitomized a blend of vulnerability and grace, with her anguish balanced by an acute sense of discipline in her performance as a goodwill ambassador for the United Nations Children's Fund (UNICEF). Jolie, by contrast, showcases through her work for the United Nations High Commissioner for Refugees (UNHCR) an eccentricity and a willingness to freelance with which Audrey Hepburn would have been most uncomfortable.

If the individual range of activity associated with the mobilization of star power has expanded, so have the collective categories that attract celebrity diplomats. Hollywood held a near monopoly over celebrity status until the 1950s and early 1960s. By the late twentieth and early twenty-first centuries, the conditions for fame had become far more diffuse. Sports figures entered the world of universal celebrity in a manner that rivals and sometimes surpasses the glamour of movie stars. The role of royalty has been recalibrated as well. Unlike Grace Kelly, Princess Diana was a massive global celebrity without appearing in movies. Indeed, the work of Princess Diana shows both the continuity and the enormous shift in the mobilization of star power. Akin to Audrey Hepburn, Princess Diana can be classified as a glamorous enthusiast of the highest rank whose activities embedded her into the world of public diplomacy.

A final point of evolutionary distinction is the blurring of the lines vis-à-vis celebrity diplomats between their public and private lives. Audrey Hepburn engaged with the diplomatic world when she no longer was doing movies. And she did so—at least in the public eye—without a partner. Although her third husband, Robert Wolders, proved extremely supportive of her work, the focus was entirely on her as a solo act. Much of the glamour and gravitas she imparted to this role derived from her ability to do it in virtual retirement. In contradistinction, many of the biggest current celebrity diplomats juggle lives as performers and as celebrity diplomats at the peak of their power of attraction. Moreover, sometimes they do it in tandem with another celebrity with whom they are in a love match. Angelina Jolie's work with refugees has most notably become intertwined with her relationship with Brad Pitt—what many have dubbed the "Brangelina" phenomenon. Princess Diana, by way of contrast, used her work as a landmines ambassador to distance herself from her entrapment in the British royal family.

These undulations in the context in which celebrity diplomats operate create new types of strains on the UN's traditional model of glamorous enthusiasts. Princess Diana could win most of her fame as an unofficial diplomat by her association with an initiative that went around the institutional structure of the UN. David Beckham—creatively connected with the UN through his work helping the victims of the 2004 Indian Ocean tsunami—went on to achieve his diplomatic moment of fame by helping win the 2012 Olympic bid for London and the UK. Hollywood actors, such as Richard Gere, do things touching on the world of geopolitics that embarrass the UN.

Still, what is equally clear, is that the same shifts opened up new opportunities for the relationship between celebrities and the UN to flourish. At a time when the UN was coming under some considerable stress, particularly from the biggest of the G8 countries, the United States and the United Kingdom, on both legitimacy and efficiency grounds, celebrity diplomats clustered largely in the Anglo-sphere provided some counterpoise to those countries' official attitudes concerning the UN. The sheer quantity of celebrities wanting to be involved as goodwill ambassadors did much to affirm the value of the UN. The thickening of ties across a wide range of tangible activities and larger-than-life personalities added to the organization's image of diversity and openness.

GLAMOROUS ENTHUSIASTS: CELEBRATED BUT CONFORMIST

The early big-name entertainers linked to the UN left a benign imprint through their performances as celebrity diplomats. Danny Kaye, the comic movie star, was highly visible in his work as the first goodwill ambassador for UNICEF. He had charm and enormous energy. His willingness to not only appear on behalf of UNICEF but to make frequent trips to disaster areas earned him the name "Mr. UNICEF" and the honor of being present when the Nobel Peace Prize was awarded to the organization in 1965. But his activities were highly conformist, engendering nothing in the way of controversy about how the UN could or should work in a more efficient or generous fashion. The same is true of the actor Sir Peter Ustinov, who also combined an engaging personality with a capacity to take on a prodigious travel and publicity schedule. The lasting impression of both individuals is of good international citizens, not as activists hungry to promote forms of transformative diplomacy.

The celebrity who stands out in her ability to define the template of UN goodwill ambassador as both glamorous enthusiast and conformist is Audrey Hepburn, the star of *Breakfast at Tiffany's, Charade, Roman Holiday,* and *My Fair Lady.* In part her reputation reflects her own background as someone who had lived as a child in Arnhem, the Netherlands, under Nazi occupation. As a wartime victim of famine, Hepburn had credibility in addressing issues of malnutrition among children and the plight of refugees that most celebrities simply did not possess. Indeed, she had been a recipient of help from the UN Relief and Rehabilitation Administration, the forerunner of UNICEF, at the end of the war. On top of this street credibility, she combined an elegance and fearlessness that evoked awe. During the late 1980s, she was willing to travel to the then Ethiopian provinces of Tigre and Eritrea by Hercules cargo plane and light aircraft. Throughout this endeavor she displayed a princess-like demeanor that had the journalists accompanying her going gaga.[2]

In hindsight, her attitude toward the political and diplomatic dynamics affecting the Ethiopian situation appears to be naïve. On key issues she refused to be drawn into controversy. Certainly, she was unwilling to take sides in the civil war between Ethiopian state officials over their admitted "overzealous and brutal" resettlement policy and the "tragedy within a tragedy" of the rebels' blockage of relief supplies.[3] In a style forecasting Bono's approach, she constantly took the high road. Akin to Bono's style as well, she cast the crisis in religious imagery. She described visiting a project to reconstruct a reservoir as a "Biblical scene."[4] On another occasion she stated that Ethiopia's lack of grain was a "God-made" injustice, adding: "I plan to have a talk with him."[5] On still another occasion she voiced this opinion: "To save a single child is a blessing ... to save millions of children is a God-given opportunity presented to us by UNICEF."[6]

The parallels with Bono are interesting to draw out in other directions. Like Bono, she moved up to icon status, and as a fundraiser she was a huge draw. During the Ethiopian crisis, a drive to raise $22 million for medicine, vaccines, and other nonfood supplies was centered on her activities. Her last mission to Somalia raised £1 million in the UK alone. As an advocate she did many of the things that Bono has concentrated on in his more recent diplomatic efforts. Hepburn sought access to the big men in the countries she targeted, including the then prime minister of Sudan, Sadiq al Mahdi. She took her activities inside the beltway in Washington, D.C. Appearing before the Senate Appropriations Subcommittee on State, Foreign Operations, and Related Programs, chaired by Senator Patrick Leahy (D-VT), she told the politicians that the worst violence in Africa is widespread poverty.[7]

And like Bono, again, Audrey Hepburn combined a concern with access to decision makers with persistence in vocalizing issues to wider publics. Aside from Ethiopia and Sudan, she made extensive visits to Central and South America and South and Southeast Asia. Throughout it all she was prepared to go about "talking my head off" and "to do as much as possible in the time that I'm still up to it."[8]

In addition to modeling the professional approach that Bono refined as part of the later wave of celebrity diplomacy, Audrey Hepburn showed off some of the emotional touches more akin to Bob Geldof. She initially commended the tremendous efforts of many Africans on the ground, (controversially) praising the Ethiopian government's relief agency as "the biggest and best in Africa."[9] But like Geldof, she also grew increasingly frustrated by the substantive obstacles in the way of the relief effort—describing the Somalia crisis as a "slice of hell" and admitting that she had had "an overdose of suffering."[10]

In her intensity of style, she was as tireless as either Bono or Geldof. She gave long interviews, not only in the print media but on TV, most notably on *Larry King Live* (taking calls for 1-800-FOR-KIDS). She read the summit declaration of a 1992 conference bringing together kings' and presidents' wives from developing countries. She fought against donor or compassion fatigue without making her activities (including the crisis-ridden, dangerous places she was pulled toward) into an elaborate photo-op. Throughout this work she used her position as a celebrity as a mechanism to shift attention from what many within the audience wanted her to talk about (her life on-screen) to the plight of children in the world. As actor Roger Moore, who followed her example to become a UN goodwill ambassador, noted: "They only wanted to talk about movies but she would not let them.... She kept on the issues that were facing children then and which still face children today."[11]

A HARD ACT TO FOLLOW

Audrey Hepburn created a model of star power expressed via the UN organizational structure that other celebrities could—and did in quite large numbers—try to follow. It was a model that allowed celebrities to go global with their enthusiasms. It linked them to UN specialized agencies, whether (as in her case) UNICEF, UNHCR, the United Nations Development Programme (UNDP), or the United Nations Development Fund for Women (UNIFEM). In this model, glamour worked to enhance the sense of commitment. No reporter who followed Hepburn around failed to mention her appearance, either to comment on her looks (elegant) or her clothes ("far from the glamour of Tiffany or the Ascot races, wearing a T-shirt and denim slacks").[12]

Hepburn was an exceedingly hard act to follow. One who tried in a somewhat different fashion was Liv Ullmann, the Norwegian actress closely associated with Ingmar Bergman's brooding movies. She became a UNICEF goodwill ambassador early in 1978. But that is where the similarities ended. In some ways Liv Ullmann can be cast as more eccentric than Audrey Hepburn. One of her early efforts was to take part in a demonstration marking UN Day in 1982, through the creation of a four-mile "human bridge of peace" stretching between the U.S. and Soviet embassies in Stockholm.

However, Ullmann can be judged as having moved past Hepburn on the criteria of autonomy. She reported on the Vietnamese boat people issue for a Norwegian NGO and then moved on to cofound the Women's Commission for Refugee Women and Children, an NGO designed to help victims of rape and malnourishment in humanitarian crises, such as the one in Bosnia during the early 1990s. In talking about this process of engagement, Liv Ullmann expressed the sort of outrage associated more with Bob Geldof than Audrey Hepburn: "We must be so outraged. We mustn't wait and talk about making resolutions; we must urgently start acting now."[13]

Other superstar celebrities found it much more difficult to follow the pathfinding route Audrey Hepburn took. Sophia Loren brought a tremendous amount of fame (she had won an Oscar for the 1960 film *Two Women*) and glamour to her role of UN goodwill ambassador for refugees. By the end of the Cold War, in the midst of the ascendancy of complex humanitarian crises, though, glamour was not enough to win kudos. Loren was criticized by reporters for turning up for her UNHCR appointment ceremony in a brown Rolls Royce that matched her fur coat. When asked how a film star like herself could help starving Somali refugees, she answered that she would lend her name to publicize the crisis. One journalist followed up this line of inquiry by asking whether she would be taking her Rolls Royce to Somalia with her. Offended—and sustained by appreciative applause by the UN staff attending the ceremony—Loren shot back: "When someone asks a question like this I don't know why you should be in this place. This is something very serious."[14]

What distinguished Audrey Hepburn from a celebrity such as Sophia Loren was precisely the mix of frontline enthusiasm (roughing it) and the ability to be effortlessly glamorous (when out in dangerous places). To her credit, Loren did tour Somalia at the same time as Hepburn. But the Italian actress gave the impression of being simply overwhelmed ("I have seen pictures of starving people on television but I never realized the situation was so incomprehensible.").[15] Unfortunately, akin to some future glamorous celebrities, the sense that her foray into the world of diplomacy seemed like a well-rehearsed publicity vehicle (a view reinforced by the fact that she was accompanied not only by representatives of the UNHCR but by a forty-five-person press team).

By way of contrast, Hepburn appeared authentic in her commitment, in that she blended her elegant looks with grace accented by a minimalist style. The media contingent that followed her was not huge. No documentaries or books were put in production alongside these activities. Her travels were not one-time events; she continually returned to war-torn spots.

The model of diplomacy that characterized these glamorous enthusiasts included well-defined gender stereotypes. Hepburn could be emotional on her travels ("Hepburn's eyes glistened with tears").[16] She could also down-play politics and highlight human suffering. She could evoke motherhood. All these images reappeared in the later coverage of Princess Diana and Angelina Jolie.

Unlike the more recent celebrity diplomats, though, Audrey Hepburn did not mix her public and private lives. References were made to her two divorces—especially the one to Mel Ferrer—but these episodes were not dwelled on in the context of her UNICEF work. What took on greater prominence was the connection between her personal tragedies and her international activities. This link was established by frequent references to her upbringing in war-torn Europe, an image of tragedy embellished through later references to her tragic struggle with cancer, and speculation after her death that she had suffered from anorexia.

As noted, Hepburn was also quite content to work within an accepted script. She did not criticize logistical delays either in her own travels or in the operations to transport food and medicine. Although she spoke out that the crisis in Sudan was "a man-made disaster," she did not point fingers or target particular actors for blame.[17]

STRAINING AGAINST CONFORMITY

The celebrities that followed Hepburn were not as compliant or as circum-spect. While adhering to some aspects of the template she pioneered, they deviated quite markedly and self-consciously in other areas. One classic case of this strain came in the challenge to the UN's position on Tibet from Richard Gere. Another, from a completely different starting point, came with Princess Diana's move to become an advocate for the anti–land mines campaign.

Richard Gere had enormous sympathy for the UN mission. Gere ap-peared with then Secretary-General Annan at a number of public events, including the Fifteenth International AIDS Conference in Bangkok in July 2004. In common with a good many other celebrities, he endorsed the UN position on the 2003 Iraq war: "If the United States marches into Iraq without the backing of the United Nations, that will be done entirely without the backing of the American people."[18]

Nonetheless, Gere's sympathy for the UN did not translate into being a conformist goodwill ambassador. Like Audrey Hepburn, he has been willing to get out into the field, focusing on a number of international trouble spots. Unlike Hepburn, he pushed issues in a controversial fashion. When he visited refugees in Macedonia with UNICEF, he wanted to get to know their situation by staying overnight at the refugee camp, a request that was denied by government officials. His enthusiasms—or an even greater sense of naïveté than Hepburn possessed—covered a far wider set of issue areas. He backed one proposal for a cease-fire and investigation of alleged war crimes in Chechnya. And he took part in the campaign to get voters out for the vote during the Palestinian Authority election in January 2005, an effort that received very few accolades. At least one political analyst based in Ramallah dismissed this intrusion as a waste of time: "Elderly Palestinians will certainly not know him and Islamic people shun Hollywood and all it stands for."[19]

It was Richard Gere's preoccupation with Tibet that brought out the full extent of his contentious relationship with the UN. China has worked hard diplomatically to isolate the Dalai Lama, who fled Tibet in 1959, from all international events, including UN forums. The counteroffensive, involving an unlikely mix of conservative politicians (Jesse Helms) and celebrities (ranging from Harrison Ford to the Beastie Boys) was led by Gere, who as chairman of the board for the International Campaign for Tibet, combined the emotional bearing and lobbying presence that Bono has taken to be the mode of operation for his own causes. In 1998, he made a high-profile visit to UN headquarters in New York in support of a small group of Tibetan hunger strikers. In 1999 he traveled to Geneva to offer backing to a U.S. resolution at the United Nations Human Rights Commission (UNHRC) criticizing the Chinese record on human rights. When the UNHRC voted to take no action, Gere stated that the Chinese had manipulated the vote: "Shame on the commission, shame on the UN for allowing this."[20]

It would be wrong to exaggerate the primacy of this campaign vis-à-vis the UN in Gere's repertoire. After all, his attacks via the Hollywood movie machine received far more publicity, from his outburst against China's occupation of Tibet at the 1993 Academy Awards to his star role in the anti-Chinese movie *Red Corner*. Still, his push against the UN was a marked departure from the standard of conformity established by Danny Kaye, Peter Ustinov, and Audrey Hepburn.

Princess Diana's links with the UN were marked by gaps not in commission but omission. In hindsight it is amazing that she was not put front and center of the UN goodwill ambassador program. If there was a natural successor to the Hepburn legacy, it was Princess Diana! As one columnist in the London *Times* noted, this scenario was not only a natural role for Diana, but it possessed advantages for the British government: "That way, Whitehall could distance itself from her should things go wrong in terms of diplomatic faux pas or some fresh scandal enveloping her."[21]

As in other spheres of her life, Diana's prowess as a diplomat was thoroughly underestimated. Within the context of the national diplomatic system, it should also be mentioned that she was stymied in her attempt to win the position she wanted after her split from Prince Charles: the role as a roving goodwill ambassador for the UK. This resistance came because the British political and diplomatic establishment was concerned about her fickleness.

Early test runs of Princess Diana in the role of goodwill ambassador for the UK produced mixed results. On the positive side was her performance in November 1995 as an unofficial ambassador for the UK in a sensitive "working visit" to Argentina, with relations between the two countries still raw from the Falklands/Malvinas war. Despite close scrutiny from the media fueled by the swell of publicity washing over from her infamous interview with the BBC's Martin Bashir (in which, among other things, she said she wanted to be known as the "Queen of Hearts"[22]), Princess Diana was viewed as a positive asset in the process of rapprochement. At the mass level, her charm offensive—mixing "glamour with compassion," in the words of one British journalist—was judged an unqualified success.[23] At the elite level, she captivated Argentinean president Carlos Menem when they met for lunch. According to one senior official, this was a diplomatic asset that needed to be cultivated: "She is charming and glamorous, and her effect on male heads of state is remarkable. Look at the Argentina visit and the impact she had on President Menem. I feel sure we could use her somewhere."[24]

On the negative side, concerns emerged about her extravagance and the mixture of her public and private lives. The cost of her outfits became an issue. On one official visit to Saudi Arabia, her dress bills—£80,000 for a trip of sixteen days' duration—caused some considerable controversy. Another issue was the impression that she put friendship before the representative function, an image consolidated by her visit to Pakistan in early 1996. Her host was Imran Khan (the then husband of Princess Diana's good friend,

Jemima Goldsmith) a celebrity in his own right as a sportsman, but also a contender for the prime ministership of Pakistan. With good relations with the government of Pakistan a priority, the trip became awkward politically.

Princess Diana spent the rest of her life showing members of the establishment how wrong they could be. In some domains her work did rub up against that of the UN, as witnessed by her role as patron of the National AIDS Trust. But for the most part, her newfound unofficial diplomatic activities skirted the UN. This sense of avoidance is especially evident in the initiative that allowed her reputation to soar on the international stage, her involvement in the anti–land mines campaign. Following Audrey Hepburn's approach, Princess Diana became the classic glamorous enthusiast on this issue. However, she took on this role in an era when there could be instant buy-in for such a project. And one when the image of a celebrity nonconformist paid dividends! The picture of Princess Diana with an Angolan land mine victim in 1997 galvanized the initiative from one owned by an impressive (but still not overwhelming) group of NGOs—with support from a cluster of secondary countries—to one that had broad-based backing from an attentive public and the mass media.

As with Hepburn, Princess Diana's clothes (a visor and capri pants on her trip to Angola, or jeans and open-necked shirt on a subsequent visit to Bosnia) formed a crucial component of her rebranding. Downplaying her elegance meshed well with the sense of her strong commitment on the front lines of functional activity. Like Hepburn, she could be emotional in the field, with a palpable sense of distress—and inclination to embrace those (particularly the young) who were suffering—for all to see when she met with victims. In addition, her repeated visits wore down any feelings of cynicism that her activities were an insincere act of self-promotion.

The British media were particularly cutting about female celebrities entering the world of diplomacy. A host of enthusiastic amateurs, including notably Bianca Jagger (the harsh critic of Bono and Geldof, who was taken to task when she changed the focus of her attention from her native country, Nicaragua, to the crisis in Bosnia) faced less than friendly fire about their intrusions into crisis areas.[25] As she became engaged in the land mines initiative, Princess Diana, unlike her exceptional predecessor Audrey Hepburn, was unavoidably drawn into this morass.

The operational difference between Princess Diana and Audrey Hepburn came in both focus and form. Unlike Hepburn, Princess Diana built up an array of connections within the NGO world, especially with the Red Cross, the HALO Trust, Oxfam, and the Mines Advisory Group. Unlike Hepburn, she used these groups rather than the UN as vehicles for her work. Princess Diana's trip to Angola was managed by the Red Cross, an organization to which she had a long but low-key connection. The coincidental advantage in locating her value in targeting the land mines campaign was self-evident. Princess Diana was enthusiastic about this choice: "This is the type of format I've been looking for."[26] A Red Cross representative in turn declared after her triumphal visit to Angola: "We were stupid not to think of this before. This is what we should have used the princess for when she was patron, rather than sticking her on those dull committees."[27]

Yet, despite this mutual endorsement, Princess Diana continued to play the field in terms of NGO commitments. Her follow-up Bosnian trip was not organized by the Red Cross (apparently because it considered this visit to be too dangerous, as it had as well with an earlier plan for Princess Diana to go to Cambodia). Rather, she worked through the more specialized Landmine Survivors Network, and the UK demining organization, Mines Advisory Group. One of the attractions of this shift in loyalty for Princess Diana was the focus these organizations had on survivors helping survivors. Another appeal was that these organizations did not set limits on the geographic boundaries of her activities. Just before she died, she asked one of the founders of this latter group, "Where should we go next?"[28]

Controversy about who owned Princess Diana's celebrity (and just as importantly, who benefited from it) inevitably spilled into the domestic political arena. The traditionalist Conservative Party remained highly suspicious of her—and indeed of almost all other celebrities. In line with earlier criticism, she was labeled by this component of the establishment as a "loose cannon," that is to say, someone who had little knowledge of the complexities on the ground.

As in her earlier forays into the diplomatic world, this resistance stalled but did not completely stop Princess Diana. She was dissuaded to appear before a UK House of Commons committee in June 1997 because of this type of criticism. But she used the setback as a further incentive to recraft her image, developing a well-trained antenna on how to turn controversy to her advantage by emphasizing her image as a humanitarian, not a political figure.

Despite these disavowals, however, her work was designed to exploit New Labour's positive obsession with celebrities as part of Tony Blair's bid to distance himself from the Conservatives and Labour's own orthodox inclinations. Less than two months after her death, the newly elected British Labour government under Blair doubled its contribution to the land mines campaign, started a training program for military/NGO cooperation in mine-clearing operations, and pushed harder in its state-based diplomacy to persuade the last resistant countries to sign onto the agreement.[29]

Beyond this gesture, the Blair government went out of its way to suggest that Princess Diana would have been granted her wish to become an informal ambassador for Britain. As recognized by Blair, the talents she deployed on the land mines initiative could be replicated on other issues. For her part, in an interview published after her death, Diana was enthralled by the election of Blair: "I think at last I will have someone who will know how to use me. He's told me he wants me to go on some missions."[30]

Embracing the Celebrity Culture: Hits and Misses

The more comprehensive embrace of celebrity culture by the UN was forged on a combination of supply and demand. The sheer volume of celebrities who were prepared to become associated with the UN through the 1990s and into the twenty-first century was extraordinary. In some ways this embrace simply extended at the global level the deepening and entangled ties between celebrity culture and domestic politics found in the administration of President Bill Clinton and replicated by Prime Minister Tony Blair. The Clinton White House was, in the words of Maureen Dowd, "extravagantly star-struck."[31] To give one compelling illustration, in a whirlwind visit to Vancouver just after he came into office, President Clinton combined a meeting with Russian president Boris Yeltsin and a meeting with a group of Hollywood celebrities, including Richard Gere (who tried to lobby Clinton about the Dalai Lama), Sharon Stone, and Richard Dreyfus. And Blair, when he came into office as prime minister, if anything, was even more celebrity-obsessed, a condition that stood out as a marked feature of New Labour politics.

Why this synergy took place in either case appears to be rooted in a desire for some psychological exchange, with the political elite wanting to become not just glamorous but to be connected with popular culture, and the entertainers wanting to be elevated into the role of serious thinkers and doers. What is less appreciated is how much the UN absorbed the same transference of celebrity culture. With the release of the disciplines of the Cold War, the UN became far more receptive to opening up its structures to nonstate actors. NGOs and business representatives (most notably, through the corporate social responsibility initiative) were provided far more room to operate. And so were celebrities. By the time of the institution's fiftieth anniversary celebrations, a full contingent of unofficial diplomats had become embedded into the UN's activities.

Kofi Annan, as secretary-general of the UN, embraced celebrity actors in the same manner as Clinton and Blair. One of the clearest themes throughout his two terms of office was a desire to galvanize celebrities—along with high-profile figures in the worlds of academia, business, and civil society—to become supporters of the UN. So tight did this relationship become that one anonymous insider noted, "The UN has become a celebrity hotel … and anyone in Hollywood who wants to show there's nothing trivial about them checks in with Kofi."[32] In part this was a defensive approach, a device designed to counterbalance both the anti-UN Republicans in the U.S. Congress and a wider sense of cynicism he detected in the public at large.[33] However, as noted by a critic of the process, this embrace of celebrities also had an expansive component by contrasting the still dominant realist logic (based on national self-interest) assumed by most states in the UN system with an idealist version of universalism.[34]

The project "Celebrity Advocacy for the New Millennium" was explicitly devoted to mobilizing support for the UN Millennium Declaration and the Millennium Development Goals. At his first meeting with UN goodwill ambassadors—Brazilian football star Ronaldo, Nobel Prize for Literature winners Nadine Gordimer and Seamus Heaney, Harry Belafonte, Peter Ustinov, and a host of Hollywood stars in attendance—Annan called them into action as activists for the Millennium Project, telling them, "You have the personality to capture the imagination of people and of policy makers alike."[35]

In principle this embrace had some considerable logic behind it. The association of the UN with cultural diversity was attractive. So was the possibility that these celebrities would produce good publicity (and more tangibly monetary resources) for the organization. What is more, celebrities appeared during the conformist stage to bring little of the downside often attributed to NGOs, in terms of intrusion on sovereignty questions and/or status within diplomatic forums.

Yet, as could have been predicted by the snapshots provided vis-à-vis the activities of Richard Gere and Princess Diana, any opening up of the UN to a cohort of celebrities would produce both hits and misses. Few, if any, of those in the cascading wave of celebrities had the attributes of a traditional glamorous enthusiast as epitomized by Audrey Hepburn. And few of those wanting to go freelance had the style, skill, or stamina to reconfigure themselves as a new model of diplomat the way that Princess Diana could.

Few of the misses need much of an explanation. A number of choices indicated poor judgment concerning personality types or the staying power of the individual celebrity. The selection of Sarah, Duchess of York ("Fergie"), as a UN goodwill ambassador with special responsibility for refugees was made amid considerable fanfare in 1993. That choice was not without its controversy from the outset, as the selection of Fergie was done at the expense of Princess Diana. The initial tasks announced for Fergie (trips to Mozambique and possibly Bosnia), were precisely in the areas where Princess Diana was to make her name. (Princess Diana was reportedly prevented from visiting Bosnia in the early 1990s because of concerns by palace officials that she would overshadow a scheduled visit by Prince Charles.) At the outset Fergie gave every indication that she would be an excellent ambassador. Not only did she have a good reputation for civic engagement from her work as the founder and life president of the UK charity Children in Crisis, but she had a flair and vigor that were very attractive. At the announcement of her appointment, Fergie stated: "I'm not just going to be a letterhead. I am very, very serious about it. I want to do much more to help. I am good at talking about things."[36]

The problem was that Fergie lacked the capacity for sustained commitment. With diminished financial resources after her divorce from Prince Andrew, she could not afford to do pro bono work for the UN. All she received for taking on the role of UN ambassador was the distinctive blue Laisser Passer (UN international passport). And even the token $1 a year she was to receive was removed because of the administrative difficulties associated with it. So Weight Watchers was Fergie's gain and the UN's loss.

A greater source of embarrassment came with the choice of pop singer Geri Halliwell ("Ginger Spice") as a UN goodwill ambassador. In style she attempted a dualistic approach akin to those of Audrey Hepburn and Princess Diana, with a contrast between the glamorous wardrobe she wore at social events and the comfortable outfit (chinos and a tailored shirt) she adopted for her UN work. Akin to Fergie, Halliwell took a robust position about her potential for promoting the UN, if in far less diplomatic language: "I am famous. And I am damn well going to use my fame positively. If I save one person's life just by awareness, I'm going to damn well do it."[37]

The barrier to her positively exploiting her role was that Ginger Spice's sense of commitment—and one can add, fame—did not stand the test of even a small amount of time. She did make one relatively high-profile trip for the United Nations Population Fund (UNFPA) to the Philippines to promote contraception and AIDS awareness, but after that foray she fell off the radar.[38] At least one official was quoted anonymously as saying that Halliwell was simply "not up to" the job of advocacy in the area of family planning.[39]

These ill-judged choices played into a sentiment that the UN was getting out of control in its efforts to catch the celebrity wave. Rather than gaining credibility for the UN, the approach was becoming a target for ridicule and devaluation.[40] Annan himself was reportedly shocked by meeting a celebrity who told him she was a UN goodwill ambassador, although he didn't know who she was.

As a result of these negative experiences, the UN ambassador program was tightened up. Meetings were organized with current ambassadors to expand the organization's oversight in terms of their humanitarian work, and efforts were made to apply stricter criteria to the selection process for new ambassadors. The manager for the goodwill ambassador program declared in 2005: "We don't name anyone anymore without a period of engagement."[41] A case in point has been the poster star for the revitalized program, Angelina Jolie, who was named an ambassador for UNHCR only after a lengthy "audition." Even after she spent three weeks in West Africa visiting refugee camps, it was only after another year's interaction with and learning about UNHCR, and UNHCR learning about her, that (in Jolie's words) they "agreed to work together and speak about it."[42]

THE JOYS OF NONCONFORMITY

Even with these efforts there is a good amount of serendipity attached to who does or does not make a first-rate ambassador for the UN. What you see is not always what you get. Michael Douglas has done a wonderful job as an advocate for limitations on arms sales and weapons of mass destruction. Susan Sarandon has been more controversial, mixing her role as a UN ambassador with NGO advocacy (World Wildlife Federation, for example) and antiwar activism. And Vanessa Redgrave has gone against stereotype, rebranding herself from her longtime association with the Palestine Liberation Organization and a British Trotskyite party to a more benign image through her extensive work for the UN as a cultural ambassador.

A similar set of contradictions extends to other categories of celebrities. One example of a celebrity who might have been a miss—in the same trajectory as Ginger Spice—is David Beckham. Although not an entertainer per se, he has moved into that world, both because of his own aura as a star footballer with global appeal (helped by the movie *Bend It Like Beckham*), his personal connection through marriage to pop star "Posh Spice," and his status as a fashion icon. When he first expressed an interest in acting as a UN ambassador—in tandem with the then Swedish manager of the English football team—the expectations for him were huge, with a spokesman for Kofi Annan commenting: "I don't know much about English football, but I do know about David Beckham and he has a huge appeal all around the world. He can appeal to a different, younger audience who might not look up to politicians. If he is going to talk about world peace then all kinds of people are more likely to listen to him."[43]

Despite many other obligations on and off the football field, Beckham has lived up to all the hype about acting as a spokesperson for the UN. In 2004 Beckham was named a UN goodwill ambassador for UNICEF and made trips to Thailand and parts of Africa. In January 2005, he headed up UNICEF's public appeal to aid the victims of the 2004 tsunami to the delight of then Executive Director Carol Bellamy: "The global TV appeal he has recorded will be enormously useful to help UNICEF meet the immediate survival needs of children. … We are also looking forward to working together with David in the long term to use his expertise as a sportsman to support our Sport for Development programme."[44]

It should be mentioned here that Beckham's diplomatic work with the UN had a ricochet effect, pulling him into the national diplomatic sphere. Working as a bid ambassador with the London Organizing Committee for the 2012 Olympic Games, Beckham has been given some considerable credit for winning the bid for the games for the UK capital. Faced with the opportunity that many International Olympic Committee (IOC) members were big soccer fans, Beckham's willingness to put his celebrity on the line for his hometown was crucial in the competition against Paris. As the London bid spokesman offered to a popular English tabloid: "David could have put his feet up and taken a less active role but he wanted to get stuck in and help as much as he could. He ended up meeting several IOC members and we believe he had a big effect. We owe him a lot."[45]

A second unlikely celebrity who has consistently championed the cause of the UN has been Ted Turner. Akin to Beckham, Turner's roots are in the sports world (having captained the winning yacht in the 1977 America's Cup race as well as being a sometime owner of the Atlanta Braves), and he had some added celebrity and controversy attached to him because of his marriage to Jane Fonda.

But his links to the entertainment world went well beyond those images. Because of his ownership of CNN, Turner had not only a deep connection with the media world but the deep pockets to indulge his philanthropic enthusiasms. Significantly, the UN became the locus of a long and caring love affair with Turner. Advocating the need for a "Third World Marshall Plan" well before the idea was in vogue, Turner turned his maverick energy level to a number of UN activities. Along with Jane Fonda, he went to Cairo to attend the UN's International Conference on Population and Development in 1994. Using his control of CNN as a lever, he ordered the channel to cover this type of event "from gavel to gavel."[46]

In 1998, the media mogul raised the stakes further by setting up the United Nations Foundation/Better World Fund and offering $1 billion to the UN over ten years for humanitarian programs—the recipients for the initial sum of $22 million being UNFPA and UNICEF. In the same year, both Turner and Fonda were selected as UN ambassadors for UNFPA (a role that found them speaking on at least one panel with Geri Halliwell). Although his material resources were sapped by the fall in value of his AOL Time Warner stock—which had bought CNN—the impact of his efforts continued to reverberate. The creation of his foundations was given some credit for loosening up U.S. congressional funds to make up the arrears of more than $1 billion owed to the UN. Further, Turner was in the forefront of a series of new global health initiatives (GHIs) supporting the campaign to eradicate polio in Africa through his own foundations and, in partnership with Vodafone, contributing to initiatives on fighting measles and HIV/AIDS. This work was significant not only as a personal contribution but also as a valuable guide to other celebrity entrepreneurs, above all Bill Gates.

The third—and most dazzling—success story of a glamorous enthusiast embracing the role of UN ambassador is Angelina Jolie. At first glance, Jolie would appear to be the opposite of Audrey Hepburn as a goodwill ambassador to UNHCR. Although Hepburn avoided controversy (including any publicity devoted to her own two divorces), Jolie reveled in an image of wild, eccentric behavior via her series of relationships with celebrity men (including two marriages and divorces of her own), multiple tattoos, and a variety of other "silly self-destructive things."[47] Yet Jolie on closer examination appears to be the logical and updated version of Hepburn in a variety of ways. Akin to Hepburn, she plays to gender stereotypes: emotional, with an overarching concern for motherhood and human suffering. In one interview she echoed the sentiments expressed by Hepburn decades before her: "I started to cry a lot ... when I first started going, because it's overwhelming, and you can't imagine that people suffer these things and continue to fight on."[48]

In terms of appeal, the essential difference was that instead of the worldly, vulnerable, and controlled glamour that Hepburn evoked, Jolie deployed her beauty as an aggressive instrument or magnet of attention, whether in Hollywood or in the arena of public affairs. Unlike Hepburn, her appeal extends across generational barriers. Hepburn's target audience excluded the young and the marginalized. Jolie's power of attraction is concentrated among those groups. One UN spokesperson accurately portrays it this way: "The people who find the UN boring—young people and teenagers who are not interested in refugee issues—adore Angelina Jolie."[49]

In similar fashion to Hepburn, Jolie is willing to take on personal risks, at least to the extent of visiting dangerous places as part of her humanitarian work. Her first adopted child (Maddox) is from Cambodia, where she has built a home, set up a wildlife sanctuary and been granted citizenship by royal decree.[50] Her second (Zahara) comes from Ethiopia. She gave birth to Brad Pitt's child (Shiloh) in Namibia amid massive publicity and related controversy. And in March 2007, she adopted a three-year-old boy (Pax) from Vietnam. Unlike Hepburn, Jolie is not associated with a few enormous emergencies (Somalia and Sudan in Hepburn's case, despite her other travels). Jolie's focus encompasses different continents and danger zones. Her sites of involvement include not only Africa and Cambodia but a wide variety of hotspots such as Chechnya (where, revealing a willingness to engage in politics after a four-day visit, she asked the Russian government not to force 80,000 refugees from Chechnya to be repatriated) and Pakistan after the 2005 earthquake.

Nor does Jolie play down her personality or emotions when visiting emergency sites on her own (or with a small group of UN officials and journalists), as demonstrated by the publication of her travel diaries.[51] She blends her public and private lives, involving her partner Brad Pitt in her UN work. To be fair, that is not entirely a leap, as Pitt (with his former wife, Jennifer Aniston) entertained the idea of taking part in a peace mission to the Middle East in 2003.[52] But as shown by their tour of Pakistan's devastated earthquake zone in November 2005, Pitt's engagement through Jolie has reached a very different level of form and intensity.

Similarly to Bono, Jolie remains both a mentor and a celebrity who continues to be mentored. She is reported to have introduced Brad Pitt to Bono's DATA operation in order to prime him for a ratcheted-up program of activity. Her mentoring comes from her association with UN-related programs. She continues to rely heavily on professionals for background material when appearing at public events. One example was the close bond she formed with the well-known economist, Professor Jeffrey Sachs, with whom she visited several Millennium Villages as part of his Millennium Promise initiative. Together they filmed an MTV documentary, *The Diary of Angelina Jolie and Dr. Jeffrey Sachs in Africa,* that details their trip to one village of this type in Kenya.[53]

The major difference between Hepburn and Jolie has less to do with where they stand on the celebrity scale—both have won Oscars—but in the temporal context of Jolie's campaigns. Notwithstanding all of Hepburn's glamour, her UN work came after she left the world of entertainment and had reached an advanced age (by Hollywood standards, at least). Jolie's work for the UN has come not just at the peak of her celebrity but in an era (with MTV, *People Magazine, Hello!* and other media outlets dedicated to celebrity coverage) when she can capitalize on it. Everything she does is reported on in immense detail. Such a real-time measure of celebrity opens up potential risks for the UN: popular opinion can turn against even the biggest of stars. Set against these risks, however, are the enormous benefits of having an of-the-moment superstar attached to and connected in the mind of the public with the UN.

In the same mold as Audrey Hepburn, Angelina Jolie has rebranded the definition of a celebrity diplomat. She has leveraged her celebrity to engage politicians at the highest rank, from comfortably attending the World Economic Forum at Davos to sitting on a panel discussion at the Clinton Global Initiative to meeting with the president of Pakistan. Unlike Hepburn, she is not at all reluctant to issue directives about what is wrong and right about global issues. She is generous with her own money, donating funds for the building of health centers in refugee camps and $1 million to help Afghan refugees. Audrey Hepburn would have been proud of these developments. Where they part ways is in the manner in which Jolie's life imitates her art, as many of her enthusiasms became intertwined with areas where she has filmed movies (Ethiopian refugee camps and Chechnya after *Beyond Borders,* Cambodia after *Lara Croft: Tomb Raider,* and Pakistan after *A Mighty Heart,* in which Jolie portrays the widow of the murdered journalist Daniel Pearl). Audrey Hepburn was too reserved to have let this mix occur.

One of the fundamental questions surrounding Angelina Jolie's activities is, Can she continue to accept the constraints of the UN in acting as a celebrity diplomat? Or will she, either through impatience or self-indulgence, break the parallelism she shares with Hepburn and move closer to the freelance model adopted by Princess Diana? Already there are signs that Angelina Jolie is succumbing to this temptation. In May 2005, she traveled to West Africa, where she met Sierra Leonean president Ahmad Tejan Kabbah and an array of nonstate actors, including members of the Truth and Reconciliation Commission established in the aftermath of the decade-long civil war. By any standard, that was an acceleration of the application of star power. Nor did she take on this mediation role wearing her UN credentials. Following the path of Princess Diana, Angelina Jolie embarked on this activity under the auspices of Witness, a New York NGO founded by activist/entertainer Peter Gabriel in 1992 that deploys video technology to highlight human rights issues.[54]

The world of celebrity diplomacy has a wide array of scripts still before it. The emergent tensions will be between the divergent roles that the celebrities are prepared to play. Will they continue to perform under the name—and the direction—of the UN? And if so, is the confinement of these activities a recipe for either mediocrity (remembering the many misses of the 1990s) or frustration (curbing the enthusiasm of the hits)? Alternatively, will the celebrities freelance or improvise in unanticipated ways? Up to a point these tensions can be tolerated, but there are limits to the room for leeway in an organization that continues to be, at its core, state-based. Richard Gere came up against this set of boundaries in taking on the Chinese government. So, as will be elaborated upon in chapter six, did another UN goodwill ambassador, Harry Belafonte, when he called President George W. Bush "the greatest terrorist in the world" while visiting President Hugo Chávez in Caracas, Venezuela.

The other revised script diverges greatly from the legacy of Audrey Hepburn. Unwilling to accept any organizational discipline—except their own—a select cohort of sophisticated celebrities have embraced the status of autonomous agents with a wider range of opportunities for their initiatives. This desire for space in terms of site and flexibility of performance was at the heart of Princess Diana's freelance diplomacy. A similar psychology may be the stimulus for a recrafting of Angelina Jolie's projects in the future. However, the exemplary case of this ramped-up form of activity comes though the figure of the twenty-first century's leading exponent of celebrity diplomacy, Bono. Other celebrity diplomats have had some potential to move beyond all the reservations about celebrities working in this arena, but because of a lack of knowledge, mental aptitude, energy, span of experience, or in the case of Princess Diana simply fortune, have fallen short of this goal. Bono, as will be detailed in Chapter 3, uniquely breaks through this set of parameters on every count.

The Bonoization
of Diplomacy?

Bono is the talisman of celebrity diplomacy. Bono stole the limelight in this larger project at the same time as he stood at the top of his game as an entertainer, with the capacity to fill arenas as the lead singer and front man for U2. His boundary-spanning role between the worlds of popular culture and diplomacy cannot be dismissed as the activity of an aging rock star desperate to hang onto fame through an opportunistic exercise. His "day" and "night" jobs have become intermingled, if not integrated in production and profile.

Bono's ability to make a great skip forward in the craft of celebrity diplomacy lies in his combination of passion with professionalism. Glamorous enthusiasts have skimmed the surface of the spheres of transnational and domestic advocacy, but Bono has managed to scale up both levels of activity. He made the transition from working as a supporter, spokesperson, and "famous face" for an established grouping via the Jubilee 2000 campaign on debt eradication to creating his own foundation and advocacy network, DATA, in 2002.[1] And while not ignoring Blair's Britain, Bono shifted his attention to lobbying the state at the heart of the global system, the United States. In doing so he navigated the traditional boundary between diplomacy and policy making, working through both international forums (most notably the G8) and the corridors of national political power.

In common with the glamorous enthusiasts examined in Chapter 2, Bono exhibits an attractive, if somewhat quirky, side (complete with designer wraparound sunglasses, leather jackets, and a taste for fine wine) that adds to his allure. Akin to this same group of glamorous enthusiasts, Bono has brought to the cause a candid emotionalism—with a strong religious sensibility—that shapes his sense of public purpose.

Bono's expanse of influence, if sometimes overblown to the point of distortion, has reached a very different stage even in comparison with other mega-personalities among the category of entrepreneurial celebrity diplomats. Ted Turner, at the apex of his commercial clout, said (it is hard to tell whether in a tongue-in-cheek manner or not) that he had considered buying an island so that he could donate money to the UN as a state representative.[2] In some commentators' minds, Bono has reached that status, from the perspective that he can already be considered a "one-man state who fills his treasury with the global currency of fame."[3]

Even accounting for some journalistic license, it is clear that Bono's power of attraction through his measure of access extends beyond the advantages accorded to all but a narrow group of state leaders. At the 2005 G8 summit in Gleneagles, Scotland, Bono had one-on-one meetings with four of the top-tier leaders: George W. Bush, Tony Blair, Gerhard Schröder (the former chancellor of Germany), and Paul Martin (the former prime minister of Canada), and postsummit contact with Jacques Chirac (the former president of France). His access to the U.S. political elite has already reached legendary proportions, both during the Clinton administration (which, given its celebrity obsession, could be expected) and the Bush administration (which, given its aversion to particular forms of celebrity culture, notably Democratic-oriented Hollywood, is far more surprising). Few politicians—never mind professional diplomats—have the kind of gateway to the range of Republican power brokers that is open to Bono, as captured by the oft-repeated remark attributed to President Bush: "Dick Cheney walked into the Oval Office" and said that "Jesse Helms wants us to listen to Bono's idea."[4]

What sets Bono aside is not just his big personality or even his sense of purpose, but his skill set and persistence. Once the doors of power brokers are unlocked, he knows how to wedge them open and capitalize on the opportunity. The image of emotional immediacy that he conveys—targeting the crisis in Africa through ONE: The Campaign to Make Poverty History—goes hand in hand with a sustained campaign of thinking, mobilization, and delivery unrecognizable from the sporadic involvement found among the glamorous enthusiasts. Politicians and their advisors may have found it hard to ignore Bono initially, simply because of the novelty and photo opportunities attached to their appearances with him. However, the value added soon became apparent as well. Not only did this association allow these same state officials to cast themselves as leaders who not only had moral sensibilities but also were responsive to popular appeals. Moreover, once this connection had been made, they found that Bono used the initial meeting to embed himself into the system. In the words of U.S. senator Dick Durbin (D-IL), Bono stands out by the ongoing nature of his engagement: "It's not unusual for members of Congress to be lobbied by stars and starlets. Usually it's a one-time stand. He's different. He clearly cares. He's clearly committed."[5]

More than any other celebrity, Bono has expanded and refined the repertoire of celebrity diplomacy. As an innovative type of diplomatic agent—to the point at which the notion of the Bonoization of diplomacy needs to be taken seriously—Bono is a hyper-illustration of earlier predictions that individuals could become formidable actors in the changing world of diplomacy. Stripped down to his essentials, Bono may with some degree of accuracy be depicted as a consummate advocate for a transnational concern. But from another perspective, Bono's mode of operation (and techniques of interface with state officials) belies this image. Very few individual advocates, or for that matter NGO representatives targeting global social issues, are able to get face time at the White House. Fewer still go on tours of Africa with cabinet members. None have the status of "bilaterals" extended to Bono at the 2005 and 2007 G8 summits in Gleneagles and Heiligendamm.

It is this embrace of the diplomatic process—and state officials—that has tilted some assessments of the Bono phenomenon away from endorsement to a more critical judgment. Even if some attacks on him are quite over the top in style—for instance, websites titled "Bono the puppet"—Bono's move to the inside and his adoption of an elite focus is not risk-free.[6] By his willingness to accommodate those at the apex of global power, Bono lays himself open to charges that he is open to manipulation. Acknowledging that he enjoys a degree of "access other people don't have," Bono himself has accepted that he can be considered "one of us that became one of them."[7]

Yet, in contradistinction to this image of an amateur being manipulated by the political establishment, Bono stands out as a master manipulator himself. Unlike his counterpart Bob Geldof, Bono has turned some of the tools in the conventional repertoire of diplomacy to his own advantage. Bono understands the power of language and communication in a technologically driven age of mass consumption. His words can soothe but they can also sting. By playing to different publics, he can take advantage of elite or personal competition to extract advantage. This approach relies heavily on exploiting rivalries and playing leaders and their advisors off each other. It is also cognizant of power asymmetries, cutting slack for the most powerful at the expense of relatively weaker actors. Seen through this less idealistic lens, Bono is as calculating as his state counterparts. The ends, albeit for a grander vision than *raison d'être*, justify the means.

BONO AS AN AMBIGUOUS DIPLOMATIC ACTOR

A hallmark of diplomacy is its reliance on creative ambiguity, necessitating some complex readings and interpretation between the lines. By this criterion Bono fits well with the orthodox world of diplomacy. In his public and private life he not only accepts but embraces ambiguity. As he has put it: "Smack in the centre of contradiction is the place to be."[8] His ample musings and reflections are distinguished by their constant questioning. His actions are similarly motivated by an allowance for multiple identities that are constantly in flux and animated by an inner struggle.

In terms of the social construction of this ambiguity, one key source is the influence of religion on Bono's worldview. Who Bono is (or at least appears to be) seems very much shaped by the fact that he is a hybrid in terms of religious background, with a Roman Catholic father and a Protestant (Church of Ireland/Episcopalian) mother. As in his music, the symbolism that Bono brings out in his public diplomacy is a synthesis between these different religious components.

Positive, if somewhat offhand references abound in Bono's conversations about both the hierarchical and ceremonial nature of the Catholic Church. Looking back to why he got involved in diplomatic activity, Bono referenced the social impact of Irish Catholicism: "I'm sure the work that I do at Jubilee 2000 and the work the band has done for Amnesty International is [from] some kind of Catholic guilt, but it's working, so we'll continue with it."[9] Indeed, one of the pivotal moments of Bono's involvement with the Jubilee campaign—and arguably in his own rebranding as a celebrity diplomat—was his meeting with Pope John Paul II, whom he praised as "a great showman as well as a great holy man."[10]

Akin to the "superstar" Pope John Paul II, Bono has built his appeal by promoting diversity. At concerts Bono has worn a headband listing the major world religions. In his public diplomatic activities he has made numerous allusions to other faiths. Even his initial connection to the Jubilee campaign was framed vis-à-vis a pluralistic appeal: "The ability to start again is enshrined in any worthy philosophy…. It's one of the reasons why I was drawn to the Jubilee 2000 idea of the poorest countries having their debts to the richest ones cancelled out."[11]

Looking at the way Bono's religiosity has played out publicly over time, however, it is actually the evangelical dimension that comes to the fore. Evangelism is an authentic part of his background, as Bono and two other members of U2 (lead guitarist David Evans or The Edge, and drummer Larry Mullen), were members of a charismatic Christian group as teenagers.[12]

Bono's connection to evangelism enhanced his power of attraction. The instrumental advantage in playing up this side of his advocacy campaign cannot be denied. Only through an awareness of a shared sense of mission and solidarity could a deeper relationship be developed with a wide array of unlikely allies, such as Jesse Helms, the long-standing arch-conservative U.S. senator (R-NC until 2002), the evangelist Billy Graham and his son Franklin, and Pat Robertson, the religious broadcaster. Bono could also tap into their expansive and influential network, as witnessed by having Olusegun Obasanjo (the then president of Nigeria and a committed Baptist) write a letter to Baptist churches across the southern states explaining the biblical principles behind debt cancellation.[13]

The spiritual strand of Bono's personal ambiguity relates to his territorial identity. Bono (or, as he was originally called, Paul Hewson) is in many respects quintessentially Irish. The name *Bono,* or more fully, *Bono Vox of O'Connell Street,* situates his upbringing, as it is borrowed from a sign for the Bonavox hearing aid company in Dublin. Speaking with his original accent, beginning his musical takeoff while still living in his hometown, Bono distanced himself and U2 from other mega-groups by creating and riding the Celtic wave. Although imbued with an immense sense of musical wanderlust, Bono described his music in local terms: "in … mysterious ways it's very Irish, the ache and melancholy in it is uniquely Irish."[14]

Sticking to his roots had advantages in Bono's branding as a celebrity diplomat. Bono could tap into the British sense of guilt, not only in terms of the Irish question (Bono once equated the African crisis with the massive nineteenth-century famine in Ireland) but in the wider postcolonial context (asking British politicians to put "right a relationship that has been so very wrong for so very long").[15] Nor in the application of his diplomacy was Bono constrained at all by any hold from the British establishment—a dynamic that played out in the case of Princess Diana and, as will be showcased in Chapter 4, Bob Geldof.

One of the many signs of Bono's adroitness was to establish equipoise between this deep-rooted localism and other multiple identities. Living for part of the year in the south of France, recording at least one of U2's albums in Berlin, and taking on an honorary knighthood from Queen Elizabeth II, Bono can be seen to represent a variant of the "new European." When targeting the EU, he exploited this image depicting his campaign as vital to the sense of "who we are as Europeans."[16] That being said, his enthusiasm for this European identity was overwhelmed by the frustrations he encountered in terms of his EU engagement. As he stated in one public outburst, he experienced some disconnect between what should be and what existed:

"I am in a band and we travel around … the world and what we pick up from our audiences is a lack of vision from Europe. People don't 'feel' Europe."[17]

By way of contrast, Bono has fully embraced the United States. As an Irish celebrity, privileging the United States held no risks for him with regard to a potential backlash at home. But—as with the religious dimension and, for that matter, U2's campaign to "break" the U.S. market—pragmatism was at least as crucial as sentiment. The fragmented and porous nature of the U.S. political system facilitated this approach. If Bono was able to get Tony Blair as the chief executive decision maker on his side in the UK, the campaign was almost won. A far more diffuse and continuous strategy was needed to achieve an equivalent outcome in the United States, encompassing Congress (including aides), the business community, faith-based groups, and the White House. And with a keen eye to the structural foundations of global politics, Bono concluded that it was the United States as a target that ultimately mattered if his campaign was to have traction.

The layers of ambiguity surrounding Bono's advocacy are augmented by where he and U2 stand on the generational ladder. Bono cut his teeth as an advocate when it was still a mark of distinction for a rock group to voice dissent. In 1985 he took part in an antiapartheid video produced by Jonathan Demme and starring Bruce Springsteen and Steven Van Zandt. He became wrapped up in the struggles in El Salvador and Nicaragua, where he and U2 toured in 1987. During the 1992–1993 Zoo TV tour of the United States, Bono conformed to this dissenting image, going so far as to try to phone the White House from onstage to lambaste the U.S. government for its policy on Central America.[18]

By the time his celebrity diplomat status took hold, Bono had distanced himself from this type of politics of protest, stating that "agitpop had to grow up."[19] The recipe for success, according to Bono, involved building a wider coalition: "The administration isn't afraid of rock stars and student activists.… But they are nervous of soccer moms and church folk."[20]

A similar transition animated Bono's bid for a global reach. Together with the other members of U2, Bono flirted with front-line activism in the 1980s, going so far as to take part in a Greenpeace direct action campaign targeting the shutdown of a nuclear reactor in the UK. But in his mind those days were now over, whatever the personal cost to his reputation. Trade-offs had to be made between a focus on activities that looked good and those that had the potential to deliver substantive results. The former was far more attractive to most people: "A rock star looks much better on a barricade with a handkerchief over his nose and a Molotov cocktail in his hand than he does with a bowler hat and brief case full of World Bank reports."[21] But in his mind the sacrifice was worth it, even if it meant taking on the character of "a policy wonk."[22]

In much of their activity—including their lobbying efforts at the Gleneagles and Heiligendamm G8 summits—Bono and Geldof have played off each other as the proverbial "good cop, bad cop," as will be elaborated upon in Chapter 4. The touchstone and original measure of Bono's stature as a celebrity diplomat, however, was clearly not Geldof but the most well-connected and tactically brilliant of the glamorous enthusiasts, Princess Diana. As early as 1999 one journalist picked up on this comparison, with an appreciation for the connection between where Princess Diana's activities had left off and Bono was going. Eyeing how Bono's style evolved through the Jubilee 2000 and the Drop the Debt campaigns, Andrew Collier made the astute comment: "It's a bit like Princess Diana and her landmines campaign. It helps to make things happen."[23]

Like Princess Diana, Bono had to deal with rebukes that his "day" and "night" jobs—even if Bono's musical day job was most often performed at night—were at odds with each other. Bono freely acknowledged that tensions existed. In the leadup to the high-stakes activities at the 2007 G8 summit, Bono openly expressed discontent (and fatigue) with his self-appointed role, taking himself away from a "rehearsal room with my band" to a life that increasingly cast him as a "pest" and a "self-righteous rock star."[24] But also in similar fashion to Princess Diana, Bono must be given enormous credit for reconfiguring the concept and action plan for celebrity diplomacy without any formal training and even very much formal education. Bono demonstrated that the craft of diplomacy could be learned in and on sites outside foreign ministries. If sometimes frustrated by the trajectory and time consumed by Bono's international advocacy, the other members of U2 could also award him full kudos for the success of his nonmusical work. As the Edge put it bluntly, "Who would know that someone who stopped his formal education at 16, and had been writing songs and touring the world as a singer, can get stuck into the body politic and be listened to on the highest levels?"[25]

THE QUINTESSENTIAL OUTSIDER-INSIDER

The rapid elevation of Bono to a position best described as that of the outsider who moved inside provides an excellent gauge of the opportunity structure available for talented and agile celebrity diplomats. As part of his manipulation of this structure, Bono exploited the fascination of political leaders (particularly those of the baby boomer generation and beyond) with entertainers and popular culture. Some, such as Tony Blair and Bill Clinton, even had pop culture pretensions (Clinton playing sax and Blair guitar; he even played in a band named The Ugly Rumours). Even those leaders with more high-brow cultural tastes, such as James Wolfensohn, the then president of the World Bank (who plays classical piano), went out of his way to meet Bono, if only, as one observer put it, because "guys with egos respond to other guys with egos."[26] This mix of factors—a narcissistic affinity with popular celebrities and a big dog mentality—created the ideal atmosphere for advocacy. Moreover, those decision makers who initially dismissed Bono (then Harvard president Larry Summers comes to mind) tended to quickly make up for that oversight so as not to look out of the cultural loop.[27] As Bono himself acknowledged, "We were pushing at an open door."[28]

Added to this opportunity structure was the skill by which Bono connected his own campaign to larger historical processes. In presenting a petition to then UN secretary-general Kofi Annan on behalf of the campaign for debt eradication, Bono proudly testified that this petition had been signed by 21.2 million people from 160 countries and constituted "the biggest grassroots movement since antiapartheid and the broadest movement of people power on the globe since Civil Rights in the sixties."[29] An extension of this theme—and an explicit attempt to balance sentiments from the liberal and conservative ends of the political divide—came with Bono's call for the development of a "national rifle association for the poor," that is to say, an organization that would combine the organizational efficiency of the NRA with the sense of purpose associated with the civil rights movement.[30]

Bono combined his society-based networking with a masterful display of state-oriented diplomacy. What Bono comprehended more than any other celebrity—although Bob Geldof shared his enthusiasm—was that the G8 created a perfect target site for his brand of public advocacy. All the key leaders could be lobbied in a discreet but focused fashion, according to the same set of deadlines and types of domestic pressure. Furthermore, key leaders of the G8 were amenable to the possibility of bending to this pressure.

Manipulating the domestic side of this process still further, Bono worked to converge apparently irreconcilable political forces. Showing that politics is about the personal, Bono juggled an ongoing friendship with Bill Clinton (he even sang at the 2004 inauguration of Clinton's presidential library in Little Rock, Arkansas) with a warm relationship with President George W. Bush. A similar balancing act was performed with regard to Tony Blair and Gordon Brown (the long-serving Chancellor of the Exchequer), whose own struggle for control of the British Labour Party has dominated UK politics, culminating in Blair's resignation and the succession by Brown in June 2007.

Bono's consummate deftness in bridging these divides is encapsulated in his address to the Labour Party convention, when he mischievously highlighted the need for both Blair and Brown to get over their differences if a constructive agenda on Africa was to be pursued. He did so through a reference to the best-known split in pop music, that of the Beatles: "I'm fond of Tony Blair and Gordon Brown. They are kind of the John and Paul of the global development stage.… But the point is, Lennon and McCartney changed my interior world—Blair and Brown can change the real world."[31]

Bono also supplemented these executive links with an extensive range of contacts among legislators, albeit highly concentrated within the United States. Those he worked with included Representative John Kasich (R-OH), then chair of the House Budget Committee, and Senator William Frist (R-TN), a cardiac surgeon and experienced traveler to Africa. The galvanizing impact of Bono's efforts, nonetheless, came to be measured almost exclusively by his unlikely bond with Jesse Helms, who, according to an aide, came to see a "halo around his head.… [Helms is] not a fan of his rock 'n' roll stuff, but he's a fan of Bono as a man."[32]

Nor did Bono leave the leaders' policy advisors alone. In the United States he assembled a solid bond with a variety of top personnel in both the Clinton and Bush administrations, including Larry Summers (President Clinton's secretary of the treasury) and Gene Sperling (Clinton's chief economic advisor) in the former and Condoleezza Rice (whom he met at the 2001 G8 summit in Genoa) and Randall Tobias (until recently the U.S. global AIDS coordinator and administrator of the U.S. Agency for International Development when he was caught up in the "D.C. Madame" scandal) in the latter.[33] In the wider context of the G8, he penetrated at least one of the sherpa meetings, which concentrated on drawing up the agenda and communiqué for the Gleneagles G8 summit.

If Bono's diplomacy mirrored the intense issue-specific flavor at the core of such initiatives as the anti–land mines campaign, it took a completely divergent turn on how best to deal with the U.S. power structure. The anti–land mines campaign tried to go around resistance, with a focus on building up support among "like-minded" allies. Bono, by way of contrast, tried to penetrate the U.S. system head on. As DATA's government relations director said: "Bono realized that he needed to play by the rules of Washington, and that's what we're doing."[34] The ongoing search for partisan balance wrapped up with this strategy can be grasped by the backgrounds of the two professionals Bono hired as lobbyists for DATA. Tom Sheridan had what might be considered the expected profile of such a lobbyist, given his previous work as a former policy director on the AIDS Action Council and connections with liberal stalwart Senator Edward Kennedy (D-MA), whose nephew Bobby Shriver (the cofounder and chair of DATA and subsequently the chief executive officer of Product Red) had been a longtime backer and go-between for Bono in navigating the corridors of Washington, D.C. Scott Hatch, by contrast, reveals the stretch of Bono's reach to the other side of the political divide. For Hatch was a former executive director of the Republican National Congressional Committee and a former aide to the controversial House majority leader, Tom DeLay (R-TX until 2006).

THE POWER OF VOICE

This emphasis on working through the domestic political/policy process highlights the mixture of profile and professionalism located within Bono's diplomacy. Bono's comparative advantage was not only gaining access to a select political elite but communicating to a much wider societal audience about the progress of his campaign.[35] In a variation of the classic dualistic international/domestic game, Bono played not only to the obsession of the political elite with celebrity culture but also to a popular media culture that would relay his messages back and forth between the elite and the mass public. One part of this game was performed in an exclusive atmosphere, and the other part became an element of an ongoing public spectacle. Indeed, at the 2007 Heiligendamm G8, Bono raised this dualistic ante another notch. His access to, and comfort level with, President Bush was fully on display on the first day of the summit. Meeting with Bono, along with Bob Geldof and Youssou N'Dour, before the start of the meeting, Bush called out: "Hanging out with good company, aren't I?"[36] On the second day, however, Bono turned his focus to grab the attention of the assembled media from the G8 leaders toward the antipoverty message delivered at a parallel celebrity press conference. Such a tactic was deemed a "redistribution of the cameras."[37]

Bono's sex appeal might not measure up to that of Hollywood stars such as Richard Gere and Angelina Jolie. Nor (aside from the sunglasses) is he usually considered a fashion icon of the same rank as Princess Diana and David Beckham. Where Bono outdid other figures was his communication skills. Bono Vox, his original nickname, meant something in terms of the application of the style and substance of celebrity diplomacy. In concert settings, Bono made superb use of his good voice in performing before huge crowds. In advocacy, Bono's voice was equally talented and compelling. The abundant powers of attraction and persuasion that Bono possessed came above all else from the power of his voice. As Bono noted in one of his many moments of self-reflection, albeit without giving credit to his own unique capacity for amplification: "It is absurd, if not obscene, that celebrity is a door that such serious issues need to pass through before politicians take note. But there it is. The idea has a force of its own. We're making it louder. Making noise is a job description, really, for a rock star."[38]

The variety of techniques through which Bono uses his voice highlights the range of his discursive repertoire. At a basic level, he used language to draw attention both to the issues he cared about and to his own role as moral entrepreneur. On both counts he was a master of sound bites. His phrasing conveyed the genuineness of his attachment to the campaign, with a central focus on Africa: "[It's] a continent bursting into flames.... We've got watering cans; when what we really need are the fire brigades."[39] He signaled from the outset that his own commitment transcended either the superficial or the provocative style associated with other celebrities. He made it clear as well that he was interested in delivery, not just gestures: "It's my job to turn up for the photograph if they're ready to cut the ribbon."[40] And even on the most sensitive issues, such as AIDS relief, his approach was a pragmatic one without ideological overtones or limitations: "If they want to paint the drugs red, white and blue, I don't care."[41]

A second focus of his communication was the gaining and processing of information. Bono made no pretense that as a nonprofessional diplomat he knew or understood all the nuances of the issues for which he was campaigning. Armed with raw enthusiasm—and akin to Princess Diana and Angelina Jolie—the supreme self-confidence that he could gain knowledge from meeting with experts and digesting the information given to him, Bono sought mentoring from a number of formidable sources. In the Jubilee campaign he was very much influenced by activist outsiders, most notably Ann Pettifor and Jamie Drummond (who became DATA's executive director). In the ONE campaign, under the coaching of political insiders such as Bobby Shriver, Bono made the shift to seeking knowledge from insiders or at least individuals with impressive public personas, such as Jeffrey Sachs. Such a dual undertaking allowed him to pick up both the language that would be valuable for public advocacy and the "technical" speak to provide him with the credibility he needed inside the Washington beltway.[42]

A third objective of Bono's discourse was to cultivate his relationships with targeted members of the political elite. This charm offensive was based on different templates. It made use of an echoing technique, in a variation of the theme developed by NGOs, by playing back the statements of a notable figure in a favorable light. This approach stood out when he met with President Thabo Mbeki and echoed the South African president's call for an African renaissance back to him: "Africa is the continent of the future. The twenty-first century is Africa's century."[43] Another method surfaced when he echoed former secretary of state Colin Powell's concerns that "the greatest weapon of mass destruction is the AIDS virus and when a military man says something like that you know you have to start paying attention."[44]

As could be anticipated from the discussion above, the range of Bono's vocal appeals—what he termed "the melody line" of his pitch—not only extended but showcased his faith-based appeal. On poverty and debt cancellation, he quoted passages from the Bible about Jesus urging his followers to help the unfortunate. As illustrated most vividly in his meeting with Senator Helms, Bono talked "about Scripture … about AIDS as the leprosy of our age."[45]

If charm served as a crucial ingredient, so was a resort to the "mobilization of shame." Bono's ultimate influence was the dispensing of positive or negative appraisals. Indeed, his initial power of attraction for the political elite was the expectation of a positive appraisal. But they did not get this seal of approval just through symbolic actions. Bono wanted results: "My job is to bring some applause if a politician is bold enough to make these new steps."[46]

When disillusioned, Bono has been quite willing to make examples of leaders who fell short of (his) expectations. A case in point was his yo-yo relationship with former Canadian prime minister Paul Martin. Galvanized by a meeting of the minds on debt relief, Bono heaped accolades on Martin through the 1990s for his "vision" and his willingness to stick "his neck out [in taking] a moral position."[47] In 2003, Bono was the guest speaker of honor at the political convention that confirmed Martin's elevation to prime minister. Yet, when Martin refused to embrace the 0.7 percent of gross national income figure for Official Development Assistance (ODA) campaigned for by Bono as part of his Africa/poverty campaign, their relationship took a dive. In the aftermath of Gleneagles, Bono was ready to put the boot to the relationship: "I'm mystified by the man…. I just think it's a huge opportunity that he's missing out on."[48]

A similar sort of swing in attitude can be seen in Bono's relationship with Paul O'Neill, George W. Bush's first secretary of the treasury. In the most bizarre episode of Bono's mission-oriented diplomacy, Bono and O'Neill agreed after a ninety-minute conversation at Davos that they would go together on a fact-finding trip to Africa in mid-2002. In doing so they showed themselves to be the proverbial odd couple. From the time they set foot in Africa, disputes on such issues as the link between the level of development assistance and the improvement in water sanitation capabilities at the local level stood out. Bono was in favor of such a linkage, whereas O'Neill, with his Wall Street background, was not. Paul Krugman recounts the disagreement: "Bono was furious, declaring that … if the secretary can't see [the linkage] we're going to have to get him a pair of glasses and a new set of ears."[49]

A fourth objective of Bono's diplomacy of voice—in between celebration and dismissal—was to nudge and cajole his central targets toward the delivery of results. In early 2003 Bono scored what appeared to be an impressive double victory. He helped extract a promise from the Bush administration not only that the ODA budget of the United States would be nearly doubled via the Millennium Challenge Account program, but also that the increase would be accompanied by the launching of a new AIDS initiative. Such announcements, nonetheless, proved difficult to translate into legislative action. Facing delay after delay, Bono kept up a vocal barrage combining positive reinforcement (stating that he believed that President Bush remained very passionate about the issue) with different types of pressure. Among the techniques Bono utilized to get his voice heard was a seven-day, seven-state Heart of America tour through the so-called red states with other celebrities such as Lance Armstrong, Ashley Judd, and Warren Buffett.

In the face of sustained delays within the U.S. political system, Bono chose to open up another front, turning his persuasive powers from Bush to Tony Blair, the host of the 2005 G8 summit. Without directly confronting the U.S. government, Bono at last borrowed from the repertoire of the proponents of the anti–land mines campaign and endeavored to go around the central site of resistance. By the end of 2004, Bono had tailored a starker message intended to resonate with the Bush administration in the post-9/11 environment, by highlighting the issue as the root cause for terrorism: "Africa is not the frontline on the war … but it could be soon."[50]

The fifth way in which Bono used his vocal power was to mentor other celebrities who might want to test the waters of celebrity diplomacy. As an enthusiastic amateur turned professional, Bono has revealed himself to be quite willing to take on the role of confidante and guide. Bono advised a number of Hollywood stars—George Clooney and Brad Pitt among them—about how they could make the jump to professional status as diplomats through the ONE campaign or other channels. On top of this, he steered a number of other entertainers in the musical world in the same direction. To give just one illustration, Alicia Keys identified Bono as her source of inspiration for taking on greater responsibilities in the public arena. Recounting how she had become so involved in the struggle against HIV/AIDS, Keys gave a great deal of credit to the U2 front man: "I had a great conversation with Bono the other day and I said: 'Tell me, just tell me how you do it. How?' The answer, as always with Bono, was a direct one: the route was 'knowledge and the allocation of time.'"[51]

THE BONOIZATION OF DIPLOMACY—
OR THE DIPLOMATIZATION OF BONO?

This extended discussion justifies an appraisal of the Bonoization of diplomacy. Bono has put a celebrity face on the processes that have been termed a unique "new" diplomacy.[52] As in the prototypical case of this innovative style of diplomacy, the anti–land mine initiative, the imperatives of speed and visibility (doing something, doing it quickly, and being seen to be doing it) stand out as the hallmark feature of Bono's global efforts.

The key point of difference between Bono and this form of new diplomacy (or more accurately, new multilateralism) remains in large part the use of his celebrity as a galvanizing tool. Even as ultimately successful as the landmines campaigns proved to be, for several years it received little media attention. Indeed, it is a now accepted view that the campaign only took off when Princess Diana lent her name and face to it. Bono's identification both with the debt cancellation issue and the ONE campaign attracted copious notice right from the outset.

Bono maximized publicity by further breaking down the worlds of entertainment and global advocacy. Audrey Hepburn completely separated her life as a movie star from her activities as a UN ambassador. Princess Diana at least tried to distance her public and private lives. Bono—often to the chagrin of his fellow band members in U2—commingled his dual personas and jobs as rock star and celebrity diplomat. The language he used as a tool of mobilization (including the religious elements) echoed some of the allusions featured in his songs. The concert stage became in essence a public platform to build support for his activist endeavors.

To emphasize the innovative nature of Bono's activities is not to neglect other, quite strikingly orthodox, features in his diplomatic toolkit. If there is a robust multilateral tendency in his repertoire, so too is there the strong, even dominant hold of bilateralism. In terms of siting, Bono's clear preference is still to meet and to negotiate with leaders or chief executives on a one-to-one basis. This predilection is apparent in both his symbolic focus on individual photo-ops and in his instrumental deal-making. In terms of mechanisms, he is quite ready to borrow from the style sheet of the best-known official diplomats, above all Henry Kissinger, as well as from the unofficial exponents of new diplomacy. This copying from traditional sources is most obvious in Bono's love of shuttle diplomacy, in which he targets individual politicians or advisors on an ongoing basis, repeatedly crossing the Atlantic to do so.

In accordance with the tenets of classic diplomacy Bono pays extraordinary heed to the need for building trust with the high-ranking public figures he targets. His emphasis on social banking, nevertheless, occurs in combination with a specific streak of calculation, even manipulation. He has played off political rivals in all the major countries at the top of his target list, whether Presidents Clinton and Bush or Prime Minister Blair and Chancellor Gordon Brown. His harsh treatment of leaders from the lower tiers of the G8 hierarchy can be contrasted to his "softly, softly" approach to those at the apex. When Paul Martin refused to meet the 0.7 percent target, Bono applied discipline. Bush's failure to deliver on either his promises of foreign aid or AIDS relief was met by frustration, but no public breaking off of the relationship.

The opportunities for such manipulative behavior increase with the expanded global reach of his activities. Bono timed the Australian leg of the Vertigo tour perfectly to coincide with the meeting of the G20 finance ministers in Melbourne at the end of November 2006. On the outside of this summit, Bono galvanized attention from all the local media outlets for the Make Poverty History agenda through numerous interviews and a "surprise" appearance at a concert that featured Pearl Jam and a number of leading Australian artists. Targeting the insiders, Bono once again played off the differences among Australian government leaders. When Prime Minister John Howard shunned a meeting, Bono went around him to target the federal Treasurer, Peter Costello, the actual host of the G20.[53] In doing so, Bono tweaked a personal connection of note: the Make Poverty History campaign's national co-chair was Tim Costello, the treasurer's brother, Baptist minister, and chief executive of World Vision Australia.

The concept of the Bonoization of diplomacy has to be intertwined with the image of the diplomatization of Bono. The commonplace interpretation is that a rock musician such as Bono is unwilling or unable to see nuances or to make compromises. At the time of the Gleneagles summit, one journalist went so far as to make a sharp cultural distinction between entertainers and diplomats on this basis: "There is no equivalent of the diplomatic fudge in pop [music]."[54]

Yet, at odds with this depiction, Bono has taken on many of the traits of the official diplomatic culture. For example, Bono obsesses over deadlines. To make things happen, though, he exhibits a degree of pragmatism absent from the stereotypes of new, unofficial diplomats. He is quite ready not only to cut corners in terms of negotiations but to make compromises. Doing what is right and doing what is necessary are not contradictory procedures to him. Different state leaders (and their officials) can be treated in a divergent manner, not because of any criteria of fairness but rather because of their discrepancies in power.

Any discussion about Bono must deal not only with the positive qualities underscoring Bono's activities but the gaps evident between his diplomatic approach and those of his peer group of other celebrity diplomats in parallel ascendancy. In large measure this comparative analysis turns on what attributes are in their repertoire. Bono privileges his voice, not material resources. Significantly, Bono finances DATA not with his own money but through contributions made by a number of well-known and well-off backers, including George Soros and Bill Gates. As will be examined in Chapter 5, this support is a key ingredient in the innovative organizational approach deployed by celebrity diplomats, stretching the network beyond entertainers to another category of participants who, although not glamorous, are certainly celebrated for their entrepreneurial acumen and massive well of material resources.

Bono remains the crucial pivot on which the entire ambit of celebrity diplomatic activities rests. Yet the full richness of this phenomenon can only be appreciated by looking to an extended range of personalities who have entered the same arena. Some of these celebrities—especially in the non-English-speaking world and within the global South—continue to be overshadowed by the exploits of Bono. Others in the North are marked by their contradistinction to him. The key point of comparison lies between Bono and those celebrities who possess massive material resources, notably Gates and Soros. In style, though, the most significant differences can be found between Bono and the figure with whom he is most often twinned, Bob Geldof. If Bono epitomizes the sophisticated, smooth end of the spectrum within celebrity diplomacy, Geldof is the embodiment of a far more abrasive variant.

Bob Geldof:
The Antidiplomat

On the face of it, any identification of Bob Geldof with diplomacy seems far-fetched, even ridiculous. Although it is hardly a stretch to consider Bono statesman-like, few would give Geldof that compliment. He communicates *at*, not in conjunction *with*, other actors. He arouses but does not mediate. Geldof's contribution, though, matters enormously to the expression of celebrity diplomacy. Yet he remains a misfit in terms of the modalities of its application. With all these characteristics in mind, therefore, Geldof is more appropriately labeled an antidiplomat.

Geldof's rawness should not be mistaken for simplicity: his loudness masks a figure of complex talents and flaws. Nowhere is this complexity better reflected than in his relationship with the world of diplomacy. Geldof is explicitly not "of" the diplomatic culture. Unlike Bono, he doesn't have the kind of speech admired by state officials and with which they feel comfortable. Unlike Bono, he hasn't walked with ease between the private and public domains of diplomacy.

Nonetheless, if he was not naturally *of* the diplomatic world, Geldof decidedly wanted to push "into" it. He courted its approval even as he acted belligerently. His major triumphs—the presentation of the Live Aid and Live 8 events, separated by a span of two decades, in 1985 and 2005—were a testimony to his sense of public spectacle as much as his organizing skills. So was his operational embrace and ritualistic endorsement of the entire Gleneagles G8 summit process.

In taking on a bigger deliberative role, however, Geldof pushed his skills beyond their limits. As he became more thoroughly engaged in the substance as opposed to the stylistic aspects of celebrity diplomacy, he was overmatched by the intricacies of diplomatic culture and processes. His deficiencies were exposed. His outsider role became exaggerated; not so much with the state leaders with whom he was putatively negotiating, but in respect to his alienation from a large segment of the societal forces for which he was once considered a champion.

NOT OF THE DIPLOMATIC CULTURE

To reveal the extent to which Geldof is not of the diplomatic culture, a quick rehearsal of the features of that culture is required. That is to say, it is necessary to pose the questions: What fundamental and interconnected qualities make up the attributes of diplomatic culture? And to what extent do Geldof's behavior and activities reflect these traits?

The first of the gaps—or even cultural clashes—centers on the physical attributes judged to be so salient in diplomacy. The ascription that continues to be commented on (and as a stereotype is ridiculed by outsiders) is the image of a diplomat as an elaborately dressed official replete with tails and a bow tie. Even by lowering the bar to the contemporary standard of business attire, Geldof has failed to measure up to this code. Although he moved quite successfully into the business world, Geldof never lost the look that he adopted as the lead singer of the Boomtown Rats circa the late 1970s and early 1980s, scruffy and unkempt both in terms of his clothes and hair. Geldof does not measure up to Bono on the scale of fashion icon, never mind the standard-bearers of celebrity diplomacy, such as Princess Diana, Richard Gere, David Beckham, Angelina Jolie, and Audrey Hepburn.

A second gap occurs on the level of diplomatic intensity. One strand at the core of the reputation of professional diplomats is their capacity for discretion. Another is a love for the application of ambiguity.[1] Both characteristics favor a cautious use of language, allowing plenty of room for interpretation. Often the unspoken words are considered to be more significant than what is actually said. And nuance is everything. One of the major "no-no's" for diplomats is to be boxed in or trapped in a statement without flexibility or space to maneuver. Geldof, in contradistinction, was a verbal machine, capable of pouring out torrents of declaratory statements when wound up on an initiative. Some of this commentary hit the mark and went a long way toward mobilizing both public and elite opinion; other remarks went over the top and generated controversy and embarrassment.

A third immense difference is the tone of discourse. A basic criterion for a successful diplomat is calmness under pressure, with the ability to lower, not raise, the temperature of debate. Colorful rhetoric may be resorted to, but it is usually done according to an accepted script. Geldof had little use for such protocols. Abandoning the niceties—and bland opaqueness—of diplomatic language, he made constant use of expletives as a mobilizing device. His X-rated cry from Live Aid in July 1985, "give us the fucking money," continued to characterize his style of delivery.

The paramount mood that overshadowed Geldof's persona was one of anger at the world—and you don't have to be a therapist to understand why this is so. As he has said himself, "The death of my mother is the central psychological fact of my life."[2] That jarring loss at an early age was not only exacerbated by the harsh treatment he received from his often absentee father but cruelly relived when his longtime lover, wife, and the mother of his children, Paula Yates, left him for another lead singer—Michael Hutchence—with an ascendant band (INXS). So tumultuous did this split become that, among other things, Geldof threw a rock through a window of the London house he had once shared with Yates.

Bono, by coincidence, shares one of these experiences, the loss of his mother during childhood. But he had the skill and good fortune to compensate for this loss, not only through religiosity but by a long and clearly very stable relationship with Ali Hewson, whom he met while still in school. Indeed, any narrative on Bono should not leave out the key fact that when Bono first went to Africa, immediately after the Live Aid concert, he did so in the company of his longtime spouse, who went with him to spend six months in a refugee camp in the north of Ethiopia.[3]

Without this type of cushion of support—or Bono's sense of spirituality—Geldof struggled against the forces of continuous pessimism and with periodic spells of immobilization, which saw him withdraw from public activity. In the mid-1990s, for example, he explained to a close confidant that his absence from the public stage was shaped by the fact that he had become "too preoccupied with the monstrous present and with a tentative future which I do not particularly relish."[4]

When released from the grip of despondency, Geldof's energy was channeled into bursts of strenuous campaigning. At his lowest point, those efforts mirrored his personal battles, as witnessed most bluntly in his support for father's rights within the UK legal/political context. More positively, Geldof was moved to shift his sense of outrage onto the global stage, first at the suffering in the great Ethiopian famine of the 1980s and then in Africa as a whole. Attracted to other people in pain (as he continued so obviously to be himself), he was able to turn his private demons into works of international public purpose.

Throughout his highly publicized campaign for Africa, Geldof's insecurities constantly fed and clashed with a huge ego. Even as he moved to the status of a fading rock star by the mid-1980s, he still craved the spotlight. As he himself acknowledged, the trigger for the campaign was that he was at home watching TV instead of touring.[5] Michael Buerk's famous BBC report on the plight of the Ethiopian refugee camps came on, and Geldof vowed to do something, a promise he kept first via the star-studded recording of "Do They Know It's Christmas" and then through the organization of Live Aid. By the 1990s he had again slipped back to the status of being a figure famous simply for being famous, a category in which no authentic celebrity wants to be placed. Under these conditions the story of Geldof's revived campaign in 2005 turned inevitably into a canvas on which his own emotional struggles, as much as those of the African continent, were to be played out.

Under the stress of activity, the clash between Geldof and diplomatic culture was heard in several directions. Railing against the "politics of niceness," Geldof wanted not only to make a provocative statement but also to achieve results.[6] The corollary to his store of anger was his impatience. Ingrained in his approach was a deep suspicion about the dangers of protracted discussions: "I don't think dialogue is always constructive; it can be an excuse for inaction. I'm used to the sophistication of your arguments, but fuck that. It's sophistry."[7]

Diplomatic culture through this lens was taken as subordinating outcomes to processes. From the outset of his public involvement, Geldof was distrustful of the heavy hand of institutional inertia. Visiting the UN in May 1986—just under a year after Live Aid—a jeans-clad Geldof expressed horror at what he saw. UN delegates were haggling over a plan of action, as part of a ten-year attempt to achieve a special session on Africa. As Geldof bluntly put it: "I don't think very much has been going on."[8]

Personal, not institutional, ownership shaped Geldof's activity. He felt no need to follow some set of standard procedures. Any loss of credibility (and income) as a professional rock musician he might incur because of the Band Aid and Live Aid initiatives was more than compensated by the attractions of entrepreneurship of a different type. In his mind the charity single "Do They Know It's Christmas" took off in sales because it conformed to a perfect recipe: "You could feel good about buying it and best of all nobody made any money out of it except the people who were dying."[9]

PUSHING INTO THE WORLD OF DIPLOMACY

Playing off against this tension between Geldof and diplomatic culture were other indications that Geldof had begun to appreciate both the symbolic and instrumental benefits of the diplomatic world. In large part it reflected a search for personal recognition. During his involvement with Live Aid, the media took to calling him "pop's roving ambassador for famine relief," credentials that were magnified amid his interaction with state leaders at Live 8.[10] In tune with this sense of elevated standing, one state official who came into contact with Geldof through this event disclaimed: "Bob is anxious to pull all these countries [as members of the G8] together in a diplomatic equivalent of Live Aid."[11] Still, beyond Geldof's concerns about his sense of mission also came to the fore.

A measure of socialization played a key role in this evolution. Certainly a tremendous leap took place between the organizational purpose of the original Band Aid/Live Aid enterprise in 1984–1985 and the Live 8 event twenty years later. The original project had a purely philanthropic orientation. Raising monies was the purpose of bringing together forty top stars of the UK rock world to record a song for the Christmas market. It was also the rationale for holding the two transatlantic Live Aid concerts at Wembley Stadium in London and Veterans Stadium in Philadelphia.

Some aspects of these ambitious activities were far from novel. After all, in 1971, George Harrison had assembled an all-star group of musicians to raise money for Bangladesh (to be administered by UNICEF) at a time of turmoil brought on by the struggle for independence and natural disasters. The distinctive breakthrough for the Band Aid/Live Aid activities came in terms of their sheer scope of organization. Taking full advantage of the introduction of infant forms of satellite technology, Geldof staged the concerts in real time for fifteen continuous hours with a near global audience of some 1.5 to 1.7 billion and what was estimated to be 93 percent of all TV sets. Donations raised via the recording and the concert were astonishingly large, to the sum of some $100 million.

By 2005 Geldof had recognized that charity was no longer enough. To tackle the problems he now identified as the core obstacles to Africa's development—aid, debt, and health issues—engagement with the official diplomatic process became necessary. Geldof therefore raised his own level of engagement with the state-based diplomatic process at the G8. Networking at the elite level became at least as important as mass mobilization.

Leadership had to be matched up with an approach designed to put Africa into the forefront of the G8 summit. Akin to Bono, Geldof targeted Tony

Blair to champion the establishment of a Commission for Africa. Blair, from Geldof's perspective, served as the perfect vehicle for delivery. Geldof remembered him as a young parliamentarian in the mid-1980s who had been influential in setting up a Band Aid cross-party parliamentary group. To get the idea for the commission off and running, Geldof peppered Blair with phone calls—and at least one breakfast meeting—on the subject of Africa from the time of the 2003 G8 summit in Evian.

From the experience of other projects of this type, most notably the Brandt Commission on North/South Relations, Geldof astutely recognized that ideas do not float freely over time. There was a narrow window of opportunity in which the agenda could be promoted. As a serving prime minister and the host of the 2005 G8 summit, Blair had an opportune moment that would be hard to replicate. The frustrations of the Brandt Commission, which saw its influence collapse with the shift toward new political leaders of a different ideological persuasion in the early 1980s (Margaret Thatcher and Ronald Reagan, most notably), could thus be avoided. Therefore, the essence of any such new endeavor on Africa was the speed with which it could be implemented (preferably in six months). Such a timeline avoided the possibility of regime change that had occurred with Brandt. As Geldof wisely acknowledged in the run-up to the 2005 G8 summit, even if he wanted to run with the project himself, the idea wasn't viable without Blair. To move without this indispensable cog was to meet the fate of the Brandt Commission: "Brandt and his commissioners ... were no longer in power. They weren't in a position to implement their recommendations. So I knew that a Live Aid commission or a Geldof report wouldn't be enough."[12]

REASONS FOR GELDOF'S PROMINENT STANDING

Geldof's prominent location in celebrity diplomacy opens up a number of puzzles. A major one relates to why Geldof was able to maintain such an elevated position—even in comparison to the talisman celebrity diplomat, Bono—when by any objective criteria there was such a huge gap between them in the fame hierarchy. Bono was on top of the "rock" pile because of his position as the leader of U2, one of the world's leading bands, and he did not need any kind of costar in order to gain access to the G8 summit process. Neither Geldof nor the Boomtown Rats had ever broken into the U.S. market. And Geldof as a solo act had fallen completely off the musical radar with his most recent endeavors (*The Vegetarians of Love* and *Deep in the Heart of Nowhere*), which seemed more a reflection of his personal predicament than that of an appetite for a mass audience.

What is more, because of his personal troubles, Geldof's involvement in African issues had been both distracted and sporadic since the 1980s. He agreed to do a documentary on the tenth anniversary of Live Aid only because his participation in this project would take him away from his domestic troubles. As he bared his soul to a UK tabloid: "I only agreed to film in Ethiopia again because of my personal problems and to get a sense of perspective. I needed to get out of it for a while. I went to Africa to clear my head."[13] It seems a cruel quirk of fate, therefore, that Geldof's reentry into the African arena came only after the successive deaths of Michael Hutchence and Paula Yates, a twin tragedy that allowed Geldof to reclaim custody of his children and regain a sense of perspective on the world around him.

Three potential answers can be put forward as to why Geldof was elevated to the status of a celebrity diplomat of the first order. The first relates to a strong loyalty or legacy factor. The connection with Geldof had been valuable to the careers of both Bono and U2. Geldof allocated a prime lyric to Bono in the hit single "Do They Know It's Christmas"—"tonight, thank God it's them instead of you"—which gave a huge boost to Bono's profile. Moreover, Bono with U2, levered their rising position to the hilt by giving a standout performance at the Live Aid concert. Professionally, therefore, Bono owed Geldof some form of quid pro quo as their positions became reversed in terms of celebrity ranking.

A second explanation centers on the way their individual styles complemented each other. Bono's halo allowed him enormous opportunities to build a broad-based coalition, one that did not forget the counterculture activists but stretched to include faith-based groups as well. Such a spread necessitated, however, a special kind of voice. Bono could utilize language designed to hector and to shame. What became off-limits to him was a discourse with a rude or insulting edge to it. Geldof filled this vacant space with gusto, providing a steady stream of sound bites that mixed thoughtful insight with attention-grabbing vulgarity. While Bono took on the role of an evangelical preacher for Africa, Geldof became the equivalent of a shock jock deploying irreverent or sometimes offensive language to attract attention.

Whether by design or default, this dualistic approach became a recognized strength of the Live 8 enterprise. Bono provided the smooth diplomacy, the strategic sense, the uplifting message, and the tenacity. Geldof provided the tactical, discordant, and raunchy edge. Although these twin tracks enhanced

Geldof's role, they did allow a breadth and interplay of styles that played well in both the media and their lobbying activities: "We play soft cop, hard cop because in the end I always lose my patience and he's always eminently reasonable."[14]

An obvious example of how Bono and Geldof juxtaposed their approaches relates to their dealings with Pope John Paul II. Bono's meeting with the Pope constituted an authentic breakthrough in Bono's standing as a celebrity diplomat, and one in which Bono combined a mix of deference (praising him as a holy man) with wit (posing with the Pope, who took Bono's trademark sunglasses in return for his rosary beads). Geldof in contradistinction made no effort to be conciliatory, never mind charming, to John Paul II, accusing the Pope on more than one occasion of being "anti-Christian" for his restrictive views on reproductive issues.[15]

A third and in some ways more compelling explanation is that Geldof mattered not because of his celebrity standing or his alternative distinctive voice, but because of his organizational experience and acumen. Like an experienced sports veteran, Geldof was brought out of semiretirement by Bono because of a very specific skill set that could not be readily reproduced by a younger cohort. Geldof's casual indifference to appearance and manners should not be taken as an indication of a scruffy or muddled mind. When focused, Geldof became razor sharp in both identifying and seizing business opportunities.

Bono's ease around politicians was matched by Geldof's comfort zone with the business side of the musical world. In both the Live Aid and Live 8 operations, he relied heavily on a team of people well-versed in the commercial dimensions of running concerts on a profitable basis, including the well-known promoter Harvey Goldsmith and impresario Maurice Oberstein. Notwithstanding his own lack of recent commercial success, Geldof was still highly regarded as a player within the very tough, masculine, and high-risk UK musical industry.

As witnessed by his experiences with Live 8, Geldof could get his way through both stroking and bullying. Less assertive personalities such as Midge Ure, the Utravox lead singer, could be used as a partner and then shoved out of the spotlight. Although Ure was instrumental in writing "Do They Know It's Christmas," he was so muscled aside by Geldof at Live Aid that there was widespread speculation that Ure and his band had been moved down the lineup so Geldof and the Boomtown Rats could perform when Prince Charles and Princess Diana were in attendance.

Full testimony to Geldof's emotive powers (or to Ure's naïve qualities) came when a variation on this theme was replayed in the context of the

Live 8 concert. Ure was given responsibility over the concert that was to be organized in Scotland, an event far closer to the actual G8 summit than the Hyde Park event that Geldof made the center of his own Live 8 performance. However, once on board, Ure was again blindsided when Geldof called (without any consultation) for a Million Man March to Edinburgh. As Ure ruefully noted: "It's just Bob being Bob. We try to rein him in but you can't control him."[16]

Geldof's bulldozer tactics were not just directed at weak individuals. An equally important feature of Geldof's skill set was the application of his creative and innovative talent to the larger business world. With two partners, he helped introduce some of the key elements of morning television in the UK, coproducing first *The Tube* and then *The Big Breakfast* for Channel 4 through Planet 24. Indeed, introducing another major bite of irony that permeates the narrative of Geldof's life, it was *The Big Breakfast* that made Paula Yates a star in her own right and allowed her to meet Hutchence. Ten Alps, the company at the core of his current commercial interests, has become increasingly diversified in its output, making Radio 5 live shows and producing TV documentaries. And to round matters out, Geldof had a major stake in Castaway Television Productions, the owner of the rights to the hit TV series *Survivor*.[17]

Geldof also pioneered multimedia techniques of presentation to a mass audience. Shortly after Live Aid, he teamed up with a BBC film crew for the documentary *With Geldof in Africa* to show how the monies raised by the record and concert were actually spent. He then parlayed this trip into a series of newspaper articles and eventually a book, to which Paul Vallely (then of the *Times*) and David Blundy contributed words and Frank Herrmann (both of the *Sunday Times*) photographs. Ten years later, and then again twenty years later, Geldof repeated elements of this exercise. Momentum toward Live 8 was established via another TV documentary, the emotional hook being Geldof's return to Africa. The Live 8 concert itself was carried live not only by the BBC and feeder stations, but by cable and satellite channels, together with AOL carrying signals on the Internet.

To play up Geldof as a master of detail is not to downplay the quirky and outrageous side of his personality. Some of his notions about how Live 8 would and should work caused more controversy than they were worth. One such idea was his call, dubbed Sail 8 in a vague allusion to the Dunkirk spirit, for a convoy of private boats to cross the British channel to pick up protesters from the continent and transport them to the UK. Another was his demand that schoolchildren be let out of classes on the day of the Live 8 concerts.

Still, even with this eccentricity, the bottom line was that Geldof retained the reputation of somebody who had the unique talent for making big events successful. Organizationally, he was ahead of his time, as his Band Aid institutional framework proved to be a harbinger of many of the same techniques developed further both by Bono and NGOs. That structure made use of NGOs, such as the Irish agency Concern, along with a committee of experts, to oversee how the money raised under his purview was to be spent. A similar appetite for detail dominated Geldof's efforts on the Live 8 project, both in terms of the musical event and the attendant lobbying of leaders. As Geldof graphically put it, whatever acumen he possessed was accompanied by sheer industry: "It's not the work of fucking ages, but it's exhausting and it's nonstop."[18]

If his private life was dominated by misfortune, Geldof's public life was guided by a strong sense of good fortune. It can be judged by the barometer of timing in terms of the activities he championed. In business he had impeccable instincts for moving in and out of business holdings, including a start-up Internet travel agency that he sold before the high-tech crash. In the public sphere he chose ideal dates for both Live Aid and Live 8. By way of comparison, Bono did not possess the luck of the Irish in his one and only bid to produce a blockbuster musical event. The idea was a good one, putting together a supergroup to sing Marvin Gaye's classic "What's Going On" as a charity fundraiser for HIV/AIDS in the regions hardest hit by the disease. The trouble was the date of the announcement, September 9, 2001, became completely overshadowed by the tragic events of September 11, with the terrorist attacks on the World Trade Center and the Pentagon.

ENTRAPPED BY THE DIPLOMATIC CULTURE?

A second puzzle concerns whether Geldof's activity represents a challenge to state-based diplomacy. At first glance Geldof's approach appears to have an affinity to the stylistic approach associated with some NGOs, especially the use of abrasive and "shaming" tactics. Over time, however, Geldof became increasingly estranged from the NGO world generally and the global justice movement specifically. In large part this sense of alienation took shape because of a perception that Geldof had moved closer to the club of state officials. Geldof was viewed as entrapped in the state-based diplomatic structure instead of challenging the status quo.

Tony Blair offered an open door through which a process of engagement with Geldof (and Bono) could take place. A good deal of this enthusiasm was stylistic in nature, the nexus between celebrities, public diplomacy, and spin being so close to Blair's heart. The allure of political attractiveness was also palpable in that such a process held out the prospect of deflecting some of the negative attention facing both Blair and the Gleneagles G8 summit. Standing out in the first category was the toxic spillover from the British government's decision to join the Coalition of the Willing in Iraq. In the second category was the still potent force of the antiglobalization and social justice movements, willing and capable of disrupting the Gleneagles summit. A further bonus for Blair was that this type of engagement served as another valuable card to differentiate him from his increasingly impatient leadership rival from within the Labour party, Chancellor of the Exchequer Gordon Brown. Indeed, Brown turned up the heat on Blair to do more on Africa through an impassioned speech he delivered in December 2004, in which he described 2005 as a "make or break year for development."[19]

Amid these heightened stakes, Blair and Brown competitively bent the pattern of official statecraft to draw Geldof in. One striking illustration of this willingness to accommodate was Blair's sanguine response to Geldof's vociferous attack on the G8 summit process when the report of the Commission for Africa or, as it became known, the "Blair Commission," was released. Instead of distancing himself from this attack, Blair conceded that Geldof might actually be right in substance if not in tone. In quite a remarkable move Blair legitimized Geldof's approach by declaring: "Because I'm a politician in a suit, I wince at the occasional word but, actually, what he said is really what I think."[20]

Brown did his best to match Blair's level of support for Geldof. When Geldof made the surprise announcement of the Million Man March to Edinburgh as part of the wider Live 8 project, the chancellor of the exchequer quickly endorsed this "Long Walk to Justice." Brown played up both the moral value of this activity and its practicality as a mobilizing tool in that it allowed the British people to play their part in persuading world leaders to sign up for a new deal for Africa.[21]

Yet Geldof's attraction to those at the apex of power should not hide who was the amateur amid professionals. Although Geldof appeared to have some initial advantages in this game, he soon became overmatched in a world that was not his own. Standing back from this dynamic, his susceptibility to entrapment was predictable, as it played into both his vulnerabilities and his strengths. Geldof wanted not only to get results but to be seen as getting those results, and to be rewarded symbolically, if not tangibly, for doing so. With a high degree of status anxiety, Geldof's search for recognition was palpable. He was quite willing to give up the remnants of his Irish identity by accepting an honorary

knighthood from Queen Elizabeth II. Although he professed to feeling uncomfortable with some of the other kudos given to him ("Saint Bob," "Mr.
Africa," the status of a Nobel Peace Prize nominee), he did not ignore them.

This need to have his ego stroked went hand in hand with Geldof's great
affinity for ritual—another mainstay of diplomacy.[22] From one angle the
Live Aid/Live 8 enterprises themselves can be visualized as massive sites
for novel forms of diplomatic ritual. The Live Aid concert, it must be mentioned in this context, started with a fanfare from the Coldstream Guards
to welcome Prince Charles and Princess Diana, who were accompanied by
Geldof, Paula Yates, and their daughter Fifi Trixibelle (who presented the
royal couple with a bouquet of flowers).

A more tangible extension of Geldof's search for validation was his association with the Commission for Africa. Although it was a very awkward
dynamic, Geldof explicitly linked himself with Blair and Brown through his
involvement in the commission. A far more agile and sophisticated Bono, in
stark comparison, kept himself free from any such formal entanglements.

The risks of engagement through the G8 process for Geldof were inevitably far higher than for Bono. Having branded himself as a provocative
antidiplomat, buying into a more orthodox script contained dangers. Embedded support for official state-based diplomacy meant a loss of autonomy.
Nevertheless, with the same energy he used for attacks, Geldof strenuously
defended his association with what he considered worthwhile initiatives
within the context of the UK-hosted summit. Geldof said early on in the
process: "At the risk of sounding complicit with the Government, both Tony
Blair and Gordon Brown have been incredibly brave and incredibly radical
so far in what they have put before the G8."[23]

THE ALIENATION OF GELDOF FROM CIVIL SOCIETY

As Geldof moved toward key components of official state-based practices,
the distance between himself and the diplomatic practices of civil society
and NGOs opened up both in terms of scope and intensity. Geldof's ac-
ceptance of the status as an insider within the G8 summit process was
juxtaposed with his shift to a marked outsider status vis-à-vis most, if not
all, representatives of the global social justice movement.

The benefits of convergence with state-based practices stand out for all to
see. Geldof, along with Bono, was accorded regular access to key G8 leaders
of a form and extent unimaginable even to the most senior diplomats within
the state-based system. Both Geldof and Bono had lengthy bilaterals with

Blair and Bush at Gleneagles, after being flown by helicopter to the summit site. Looking at their body language, Geldof and Bono seemed more at ease with Blair and Bush than did some of the other leaders.

But these privileges came at a cost, especially so for Geldof. Although he had built links to some NGOs, Geldof never developed the same kind of range or closeness of links with civil society or NGO communities that Bono had possessed through the Jubilee campaign and other groups, ranging from Amnesty International to Greenpeace. By temperament Geldof was a self-styled, independent-minded norm entrepreneur. He made tactical arrangements with few, if any, long-term coalition-oriented partnerships. As noted above, several of his trips to Africa were sponsored by UK media outlets, whether the BBC or particular newspapers. Another trip was organized through UNICEF, an organization for which Geldof's older sister worked. All of these relationships had the air of convenience as opposed to that of commitment.

This absence was in part a generational gap. When Geldof embarked on the Live Aid enterprise, there were few NGOs acting as witnesses to the Ethiopian famine. As mentioned, the crisis was put on the global radar by the media, not by aid workers. Geldof saw himself as playing both a moral and entrepreneurial role. He was not just raising awareness; he was helping to solve the problem with hands-on activities such as the deployment of Live Aid cargo ships to expedite the relief operation.

In operational terms, the charges against Geldof and Live Aid become far more serious. Some NGO representatives who were on the ground during the Ethiopian crisis considered his initiatives to have propped up the odious government of Mengistu Haile Mariam and the Dergue by mobilizing food as a weapon. Money and material meant for the victims was siphoned off for both private and military gain as part of a strategy of manipulation to bolster the regime. Rony Brauman, the former head of the Médecins sans Frontières, an NGO that had pulled its personnel out of Ethiopia in protest, still seethed in indignation with Geldof decades after: "Bob Geldof had come to Ethiopia. This concert, this nice operation with all the big people in the world meeting to express their nice feelings for the destitute and starving and the dying children and so on, this is just bullshit. I am still angry at him 15 years later, because at that time the aid was turned against the people of Ethiopia."[24]

By 2005, the organizational landscape had been completely transformed, with a dense NGO network operating both as fund-raisers and front-line operatives. Geldof's highly impulsive style fit poorly into this extended architecture. Geldof's personal agenda was paramount, with little or no consideration made to the other 450 or so groups that had been mobilized into the Make Poverty History coalition. The most obvious illustration of this approach came in the timing of the twin pillars of Geldof's Live 8 enterprise. The date of Live 8, July 2, 2005, ran up against the mass gathering scheduled for the same date that was supposed to be the largest-ever demonstration in the UK against global poverty. His unilateral call for the Million Man March to Edinburgh on July 6 also clashed with the plans of the social justice movement, as that date was the first day of the actual G8 summit, prime time for a major rally of protest.

Geldof remained a genius of public relations both for the event he was publicizing and for himself. His ability to use emotionally raw imagery to get attention was unsurpassed even by highly dedicated and savvy NGOs. His original collaborator on Live Aid hit the nail on the head in describing this talent of Geldof's: "He could see the mad, passionate, articulate sound bite thing in a way I couldn't."[25]

For NGOs without big publicity machines or simply suspicious of the message he was promoting, Geldof was interpreted as a vain interloper, sucking up publicity and shifting the spotlight. Andrew Simms, the policy director of the New Economics Foundation, formerly at Christian Aid, assessed the overall impact of celebrities: "It's almost always the case that the celebrity becomes the story rather than shedding light on the story."[26]

For better-funded groups, such as Oxfam UK, the challenge was quite different. Akin to Geldof, that component of the NGO world was media-driven, with well-honed techniques for fund-raising. Their mainstay was a mix of media-friendly slogans and symbols (the white rubber wristbands with the words "Make Poverty History" on them). An NGO such as Oxfam UK was also highly conscious of the advantages of access to the power centers, along with a more accommodating approach to issues of global poverty.[27]

The difficulty with Geldof for a group such as Oxfam UK was not the cult of personality per se but his tendency to improvise with respect to a script. These differences emerged at one end of the continuum regarding the record of the Bush administration on aid policy. Along with Bono, Geldof continued to cast this record in highly positive terms, showcasing it as being far more generous than the EU's. Justin Forsyth, then Oxfam UK director of campaigns and later a special advisor for Tony Blair, pushed back with a detailed assessment of all the faults of the United States in the aid and trade arena.[28]

Geldof's shifts in position on Africa exacerbated the situation. Geldof issued a continuous stream of sound bites about Africa's problems and potential solutions. On one occasion he declared himself "bored" with Africa because of the slowness in the reform agenda within the continent. On other occasions he appeared to be spending more time defending his personal legacy than working with other groups. When asked about alternative forms of intervention, he responded: "I know this shit. I've known it for 20 years. I know what I'm talking about."[29]

One of the few episodes in which Geldof felt the necessity to do a volte-face came when he attacked President Yoweri Musevini of Uganda ("Your time is up, go away") for changing the constitution to allow him to extend his rule. The miscalculation that Geldof made was that Musevini was not regarded in the NGO community as another Robert Mugabe (whom Geldof had also previously attacked).[30] Facing a backlash because of this intrusion, Geldof actually sought Musevini out at the September 2005 UN Millennium Development Goals summit in New York to try to make amends.

The continuous shifting of the script proved highly sensitive as Live 8 intersected with the Gleneagles G8 summit. The mix of accommodation and righteousness eroded a good deal of Geldof's credibility even before the summit started. Yet given Geldof's legacy and powers of access, few NGO representatives, even on the resistance-minded end of the spectrum, wanted to take him on in public. The judgment made by those willing to go on record was that Geldof's contribution had to be balanced between his ability to focus attention on Africa and his reluctance to extend his agenda to embrace issues beyond providing better aid, dropping the debt burden, and easing trade restrictions.[31]

What most diminished Geldof's standing within the NGO community were two critical decisions that he made about the Live 8/Gleneagles G8 summit process. The first of these decisions, which will be discussed more fully in Chapter 6, about gaps or bias in the composition of celebrity diplomats, concerned the lineup of artists for the Hyde Park concert. Instead of going global with a fully international cast of musicians, Geldof and his advisors chose a reprise of the formula that had worked at Live Aid. Nostalgia for the heyday of UK-centric stadium rock trumped universal vitality and diversity.

Such an exclusionary ambit—musical apartheid, as it was termed—brought larger criticisms to Geldof's agenda out into the open not only from UK-based NGOs but from African civil society activists. Paternalism was no longer given a free pass, as it had been during the Live Aid initiative. The degree of estrangement is captured in the words of Kofi Mawuli Klu of the Forum of African Human Rights Defenders: "[Geldof] has acted in his own selfish interests. It was all about self-promotion, about usurping the place of Africans. His message was 'shut up and watch me.'"[32]

The act that marked the line in the sand concerning Geldof's disconnect with societal groups, however, was his decision to endorse the Gleneagles communiqué as "mission accomplished" (with a mark of 10 out of 10 for the doubling of aid and 8 of 10 for debt relief). For many of the smaller NGOs, this decision was simply a case of flying too close to the sun of official statecraft. One NGO representative was quoted: "He got too close to the government, and he got burned." In the same vein, another activist added: "Mr. Geldof has become too close to the decision makers to take an objective view of what has been achieved at this summit."[33]

For the larger, more accommodation-oriented NGOs such as Oxfam UK, the issue had as much to do with style as substance. Like Geldof, these NGOs had become embedded in the official diplomatic process, becoming the targets of criticism themselves. In assessing this mix of results, they could take some comfort that the campaign centered on the Gleneagles G8 summit process—with the help of Geldof and Bono—had produced sustained pressure on governments and that this momentum could be built on in the future. The issue was whether Geldof had really been a useful asset in the ongoing campaign.[34]

According to the well-rehearsed script along the lines of the good cop/bad cop analogy, it may be speculated that Geldof should have been the celebrity diplomat who called the leaders of the G8 out for not getting it completely right in terms of the Gleneagles communiqué. Bono should have then firmly but gently coaxed this group to ratchet up the advances to another stage. By reversing those roles, Geldof wrote himself out as a vital player of the ongoing drama. Geldof's main worth for society groups was his ability as a provocative master of spin. When he diluted this emotional appeal, the attraction faded, as witnessed by the reluctance of any of the large NGOs to come to his defense amid the fallout from the Gleneagles G8 summit.

GELDOF'S MIXED LEGACY

It is easy to view Geldof's impulsive (and sometimes petulant) variation of celebrity diplomacy in stark, even cartoonish, terms. By acceptable standards of personal grooming and body and spoken language, Geldof was an outsider. Through his bouts of melancholy intermingled with bursts of intense enthusiasm, Geldof pushed the limits of diplomacy to the point at which it is more appropriate to consider him an antidiplomat. Unlike the other celebrity diplomats examined in this book, Geldof made few, if any, concessions to the culture of diplomacy, refusing at least stylistically to play by any rules but his own.

Because of his verve and nerve, Geldof was able to play many aspects of this diplomatic game surprisingly skillfully. The expression *entrepreneurial diplomacy* suits him well. By sheer power of personality he was able to stretch the boundaries of his repertoire from activity focused on charity/relief efforts to a massive public campaign to change the policies of the core G8 states and their leaders. In doing so, he was way ahead of the curve in appreciating how a different form of market could be shaped by a dramatic and issue-specific message.[35]

Yet if Geldof's skill set was striking, so were his own idiosyncratic limitations. Bono can be cast as the quintessential long-distance runner of celebrity diplomacy, constantly in training, adapting and pushing his own limits. Whereas Geldof is more the sprinter, very good on the takeoff, hard-driving with a big attitude, and on the track for short periods of time.

All of this flash and risk orientation served Geldof well as long as the agenda remained a lean one, with the objective being measured by sheer pulling power, both at the Live 8 concert in Hyde Park (and around the world) and on the march to Edinburgh. Where the mark of an enthusiastic amateur was revealed was when Geldof engaged and became absorbed in a much wider set of policy items concerning the Gleneagles G8 summit agenda. In this context Geldof was obviously in over his head, manipulated as opposed to being a manipulator, unable to effectively shape the agenda of Tony Blair, never mind that of the other G8 leaders, in a manner that could be accepted by his expanding group of detractors as making a difference. Stephen Lewis (a longtime activist and former UN special envoy for HIV/AIDS in Africa) spoke for many within civil society when he attacked Geldof in the fiercest of terms: "The problem for Geldof lay in his incestuous proximity to government. ... It's not an unusual process, this exercise in self-hypnosis; you get caught up in the sense of power and excitement and influence, and lose perspective. But in this instance, there's too much at stake to submit to the blandishments of rock stars, whatever their celebrity status."[36]

The Geldof narrative ends with as much of a whimper as a bang. His personal agency could facilitate a more accessible framing of the issues around African poverty. But his one-man band could not deliver on what Geldof had believed himself—and sold to others—that the Gleneagles G8 summit would deliver a big and decisive result. If celebrity diplomacy is to make a giant leap forward in terms of its credibility and operational sustainability, it needs to go beyond the individual star turn epitomized by Geldof-centered types of activities. Bono's ventures hold far more promise, not only due to his global reach but because of his hub stature in a diverse network that links exciting elements from the entertainment world with the monetary resources from key celebrity entrepreneurs. It is to this blending of material bite with glamorous buzz that the book now turns.

☆ 5 ☆

Davos: Mixing Glamorous Buzz with Material Bite

The World Economic Forum (WEF) in the Swiss mountain town of Davos is most commonly viewed as a narrowly framed and restrictive annual event. The site is taken to be the exemplar of a hyper-driven globalized capitalism in which the disciplined model of a competitive ethos trumps all else. The participants are identified as members of the top layer of the world's economic elite driving the process of market-driven globalization.

The best-known criticisms of the Davos culture—and the ascendancy of the so-called Davos man—are reactions to this image. Transnational antiglobalizers, or social justice advocates, condemn Davos as both an insidious and defective site. The menu on offer is simply a variant of orthodox neoliberalism with a rigid focus on getting incentives right in the marketplace, with the inevitability of differentiated outcomes between winners and losers. Defenders of nationalism—and national interests—bemoan the "stateless" attributes of Davos. The stalwart of this latter camp continues to be the Harvard University professor Samuel Huntington, who wrote that the homogeneous ethos of Davos (or more accurately, "Davos culture") stripped away territorial loyalties at the elite level without an appreciation of the array of cultural differentiation at the mass level.[1]

70

DAVOS AND DIPLOMACY

Diplomacy enters the picture as one of the supposed collateral casualties of the power of Davos. The *Economist* magazine jumped out in front of this interpretation with a 1997 editorial announcing the death of diplomacy![2] In distinctive UK terms, it amounted to the triumph of the Davos man over what the *Economist* called the "Chatham House man." Best known across the Atlantic for its association with Chatham House rules (whereby reporting is allowed at meetings on the proviso that no attribution is made to specific speakers), it was the home of the London-based Royal Institute of International Affairs, where practitioners and scholars of diplomacy met to discuss the global issues of the day.

To the *Economist*, this shift away from the traditional elite was not only to be expected but desired. Diplomats had become stuck in the past. With their inflated claims of knowledge about global issues, combined with a stuffy and complacent style in dealing with them, diplomats deserved, according to the *Economist,* to be marginalized. By way of contrast, the Davos man was put on a pedestal in terms of his reconfigured location within the global architecture. Comfortable with innovation, especially with respect to the new tools of communication, agile in movement around the world, and aware of all the latest trends in advertising and high-end consumerism, this new breed was taken to represent and be in control of the future.

This assessment by the *Economist* spoke to a strong sense of anxiety about the eroded status of diplomacy in the post–Cold War era. So embedded was the declinist mentality that it was not so much whether but why this (even terminal) condition had taken hold that was debated. Those who preferred structural explanations placed greater weight on the challenges clustered around the interconnected forces of technology, communication, and globalization. The promoters of agency in turn attributed the decline to the diplomats' own internal deficiencies, especially their preference for trying to exist in a "hermetically sealed world."[3]

Yet, to borrow the memorable words of Mark Twain, the announcement of the death of diplomacy has been much exaggerated. Without question, the central institutional pillars of diplomacy remain under stress. Professional diplomats have also undergone a significant erosion of their bureaucratic status. These changes, however, do not signify the termination of diplomacy. On the contrary, a comprehensive case can be made that diplomacy—encompassing a wider cast of diplomats beyond officially endorsed state actors—has never been more vital for global affairs than it is at the beginning of the twenty-first century. Numerous signs of a rich adaptation in the form, scope, and intensity of diplomatic activity belie the declinist mentality.

Davos fits squarely into this process of diplomatic adjustment. As a venue, it highlights the loss of standing for professional diplomats housed within foreign ministries. That cohort receives no special place in the proceedings at Davos. If the standing of professional diplomats as a guild is downplayed, however, the role of diplomacy as a multilayered dynamic is highly privileged at Davos. In terms of substance, its informality has allowed some sensitive issues to be handled on its margins. But the desire of Davos to be at the center of attention also opened up an emergent dynamic, with the WEF becoming resited as the prime location for the projection of the public face of celebrity diplomacy.

Davos reveals the immense capacity of diplomacy to adjust when and where there is a need to do so. As official diplomacy became more centralized, with political leaders wanting to grab the spotlight on high-profile initiatives, it became a primary venue of choice. But Davos was not simply a receptor for these changes. It could also push the evolving dynamics of diplomacy to fit its own needs. Above all, it could use the imprint of celebrity diplomacy to help rescue itself from its narrow technocratic image that over time had shifted from being a comparative branding advantage to considerable onerous baggage.

So long as the new economy—epitomized by the high-tech boom—powered along, the original menu of Davos was highly palatable. The problem came when the political/economic atmosphere was transformed in a manner that threatened to pull down the "temple of capitalist narcissism."[4] The Asian financial crisis of 1997–1998, the dot.com crash, and the massive financial and accounting scandals involving Enron, WorldCom, and other companies were bad enough. But the tragedy of 9/11 and the buildup to the Iraq war exacerbated matters tremendously. All of the "isms" that were anathema to Davos came back onto the global agenda with a vengeance: nationalism, unilateralism, and terrorism.

Moreover, Davos was not only judged to be wrong in its economic calculations, it was also seen as being out of sync with geopolitical realities. The danger for Davos and for its highly successful originator, Klaus Schwab (who had started the event in 1971 as the European Management Forum before switching the name in 1987) was that this site would go from being the subject of intense contestation as an elite and normatively compromised project to being a venue of insignificance and/or ridicule. Davos could live—albeit uncomfortably—with its critics from alternative forums, including the World Social Forum (WSF). It could not survive, though, if judged to be irrelevant.[5] Sensing this vulnerability, critics on the outside honed in on this theme. Public intellectuals such as John Ralston Saul were derisive of Davos, declaring its concept out of date as hyper-globalization became discredited. In his words, while "Classic plays have their fool, globalization had Davos."[6] A writer from the bible of counterculture, the *Village Voice*, added his own mocking kick to Davos, through the charge that the transformation in global fundamentals "makes the World Economic Forum look like a dinosaur from a bubbly time."[7]

Rescuing Davos meant recovering the aura of excitement associated with the event. From its outset, Davos has been star-struck. A good part of its appeal came through the production of the type of celebrities that its core constituency wanted to see and hear. As one participant judged, the stakes in getting the right mix were high: "The World Economic Forum still lives or dies on the buzz generated by Davos … particularly [it is] the celebrities and newsmakers who give Davos its extra dash of glamour. 'It's a matter of survival. If it was a series of middling leaders from African countries the CEOs would reconsider their involvement.'"[8]

One component of this approach was to place the accent on those prominent members of the business community who could combine buzz with the attributes of commercial bite. Faced with the shakeouts of the high-tech bust and the financial crises at the end of the twentieth century, this cohort was made up of only a few rare individuals, the dominant figures being Bill Gates and George Soros. Although many high-flying CEOs attended Davos, it is only these two that took on a profile within the Davos orbit that meshed with the model of celebrity diplomacy.

With the consolidation of stars from the business elite came a stretching out of the categories of other celebrities who took part in this forum. Davos was resited to accommodate different sources of glamour that contributed to the atmosphere of buzz. In any analysis of this resiting, a thorough appreciation of the contribution of stars, whether from Hollywood or the world of rock music, is necessary. The sustainability of Davos hinged on the unanticipated but highly effective blending of voice and material capabilities, stylistic performances, and operational delivery.

Davos as a Site of Diplomatic Theater

Through this extended lens, the distinctive feature of Davos is not its mantra of economic orthodoxy but the degree to which it has become a multifaceted hub of diplomatic theater.[9] As in the U.S. and UK national systems, a good part of this theatrical component came in a process of transference between different streams of elites. One huge comparative advantage possessed by Davos was its ability to act as a convenient site for political leaders to interact with the business elite. Another was its capability to add celebrities from the world of entertainment into the mix. The top economic leaders that formed its core membership got a reflected glow from commingling with stars from the world of entertainment. And glamorous celebrities in return could take on a greater gravitas as players on targeted policy agenda items.

From the contingent of political leaders, the most celebrated Davos man of all was Bill Clinton. With the dual personality of the ultimate alpha male and policy wonk, Clinton proved the perfect fit for the event. He was a regular star attraction on public panels. And he attended private events such as the "Friday Nightcap" session at the 21 Club, when the WEF was transferred to the Waldorf-Astoria in New York City in 2002 out of respect for the victims of 9/11 and to show solidarity with the city. Clinton's only competitor with respect to aura was Nelson Mandela, a regular attendee at Davos since 1991, when he made a major confidence-building speech. Mandela's first public appearance outside South Africa with his negotiating partners F. W. de Klerk and Zulu Chief Mangosuthu Buthelezi was actually made at the WEF in 1992. Although maintaining his status as a diplomatic superstar, Mandela's physical presence at this event trailed off after his retirement.

The various forms of mediatory activities on the margins of Davos provided another form of drama, as the aforementioned South African case illustrates. In some cases, deals were struck between domestic power brokers, most notably when Russia's business barons sealed a pact to support President Boris Yeltsin's reelection in 1996. In other cases, the focus was on more classic attempts to use Davos as a neutral site with respect to interstate negotiations. Greece and Turkey produced the so-called Davos Declaration in 1988 in an attempt to step back from war. Although the informal attributes of Davos proved a valuable commodity, in some cases the sense of drama became overheated. The opportunities for both constructive efforts and disruptive theatrical displays at Davos were illustrated in the attempts to deal with questions about the Middle East. Specific measures of agreement could be advanced, as witnessed by the 1994 draft agreement on access to the Gaza Strip and Jericho. Such arrangements, it must be mentioned, were finalized after private meetings between Israeli foreign minister Shimon Peres and PLO chairman Yasser Arafat. Yet in WEF public events, any image of mediation was subordinated to estrangement. While on stage in 2001 with Peres, Arafat took the opportunity to initiate a long denouncement of Israel. Peres retorted: "I came prepared for a wedding, not a divorce."[10]

An additional type of diplomatic spectacle came with the utilization of Davos as a site through which new promarket leaders could be introduced to the global business community. As John Ralston Saul suggests, there was an element of courtship to that activity, as the new leaders sought to build confidence with investors.[11] An air of celebration, nonetheless, flavored the process as well. On script a leader such as Victor Yushchenko, the newly elected president of Ukraine, did seek to cultivate the business community when he first appeared at Davos in 2005. But he was feted in turn by the Davos crowd for his role as the leader of the Orange Revolution. A tangible sign of his elevated status can be gleaned by the fact that Yushchenko was given the rare honor of presenting a keynote address at the 2005 event.

A still further element of spectacle was provided by the integration of Davos into the public diplomacy campaigns engaged in by prominent leaders. The most obvious attempt to use Davos for rebranding purposes came with Tony Blair's performance at the 2005 meeting. Laying claim to a slot in the program that had been allocated to his rival in the British Labour Party, Gordon Brown, Blair pushed hard to reposition himself as the champion of a justice-oriented mode of globalization.

Consistent with this accent on spectacle, Davos has adopted a very different approach to publicity than other, older sites associated with the practice of diplomacy. Forums such as the Trilateral Commission and the Bilderberg group make a virtue of the traditional obsession with secrecy held by professional diplomats. To the delight of conspiracy theorists, these forums are held off-camera, with little or no concern for public relations. As with the clubs of the older generation with which they are associated—the Rockefellers, above all else—conversations are held in discreet settings with equally discreet, informal rules about leaking information. Media barons may attend, but working journalists following these events have a hard time sketching the details of the meeting.

Davos does have an element of privacy attached to it, as some events are closed to the media. However, the overall ethos is one of generating participation and publicity. As Gareth Evans, the president and chief executive officer (CEO) of the International Crisis Group and the former foreign minister of Australia, argues, communication has been the key to success at Davos: "It's a place to get a message across—it's a way to give profile to major issues."[12] Although the conversation at Davos, like that at the Trilateral Commission and the Bilderberg group, retains a top-down bias, the elite composition and mentality of Davos departs from the standard insider-driven model in a number of ways. Access to Davos is both by invitation and through an extensive pool of executives from some 1,000 member firms.[13] If still exclusive (and costly, with hefty attendance fees), this type of entry at least opens the door to some "new" ascendant participants in areas such as information technology.

The presence of both print and various forms of online media reinforces this image of relative openness. All the major newspapers around the world cover Davos, often to the point of saturation. The *New York Times,* for example, has up to twelve journalists covering the annual event. Some of these commentators have become celebrities in their own right, such as Thomas Friedman, whose book *The World Is Flat* focuses on themes close to the hearts and minds of many within the global business community.[14] Not only does the World Economic Forum keep a sophisticated website, but Davos is extensively blogged about. Although Davos has tried to set rules of conduct about reporting—ironically abiding by the Chatham House rules themselves—this type of measure has become ineffectual. Some of the implications of this dynamic were made clear when the head of CNN News was forced to resign because of comments he made under these same Chatham House rules at Davos, remarks that implied that U.S. troops in Iraq had license to fire at journalists on the front lines.

All these snapshots are pertinent to an understanding of the resiting process with regard to Davos. In fostering the culture of spectacle, Davos has moved to erode the differentiation between categories of celebrities. As noted in Chapter 1, exceptional professional diplomats such as Henry Kissinger could become celebrities in their own right, pursuing not only public fame but a wide number of female Hollywood celebrities (or at least mini-celebrities, most of whom have now faded into distant memory). Still, what Kissinger refrained from doing was to mix the categories in any coherent fashion. He might introduce Hollywood stars to state leaders and boast about his address book at sites of diplomatic negotiation (as he did when he delivered the terms of the Vietnam peace treaty to his allies in Saigon). But the bottom line was that Kissinger saw these worlds as being completely apart. The world of diplomacy was a serious one, with stakes to match. Hollywood served as a beautiful distraction. Whether entirely serious or not, he is quoted as stating: "I like Hollywood starlets. They are even greater egomaniacs than me. They talk about themselves all the time and I don't have to talk about myself."[15]

The novelty of Davos has been to mix and match celebrities from diverse professional backgrounds and to connect some aspects of their worlds.

Although the CEOs, and indeed other attendees, wanted to meet their peer group at Davos, they also wanted to be excited and engaged by big ideas and personas from other walks of life. Davos could do that as a one-stop shop, mixing buzz and bite. Sir Martin Sorrell, the chief executive of the WPP Group (the world's largest advertising agency), captures the essence of this comparative advantage from an instrumental point of view: Davos is "incredibly efficient because so many people are there."[16] And from a more personal perspective, Wangari Maathai, the Kenyan deputy environment minister and 2004 Nobel Peace Prize winner, added: "You can bump into all these people you wouldn't normally meet, like presidents, royalty and celebrities."[17]

ADDING BUZZ TO DAVOS

The critic Jeff Faux refers to the "Party of Davos."[18] As at any party, a key ingredient is to draw people who find each other interesting and attractive. Inevitably there will be an exclusive feel to any event that encompasses the global business elite. Yet any event that includes only the top echelon of corporate executives, whatever their level of material wealth, will not generate a buzz (or a sense of party envy among those excluded).

The presence of celebrities becomes indispensable for reinforcing the reputation of Davos as the world's hottest party for high achievers as opposed to a "secret cabal." At one level stars simply add a highly visible—and often a highly photogenic—element to the proceedings. Reporters from established media outlets could sometimes offer a bemused take on the shift in style: "It is billed as the World Economic Forum but at times … [Davos] has felt more like an Alpine version of the Oscars."[19] But bloggers especially embraced the celebrities, up close and personal, with an enthusiasm that became infectious. Here is the real-time perspective of one, Jay Nordlinger: "We have Sharon Stone. Richard Gere, Sharon Stone—did I mention Sharon Stone? Angelina Jolie. Peter Gabriel, Angelina Jolie—did I mention Angelina Jolie?"[20] A taste of superficiality hovers over this activity. "Lookism" no doubt played a part in drawing an overflow crowd to a press conference conducted by Angelina Jolie in 2005, when a speech by the EU Commission president José Manuel Barroso pulled only a scattered audience. The attractiveness of celebrities, however, should not hide their instrumental value to Davos in resiting itself.

One allure of Jolie and the other celebrity diplomats came from a sensation of newness. They were exciting by default. A speaker such as Barroso offered the same old material and style. As one journalist from the *New York Times* remarked, after attending the talk on EU economic reform, he could understand why participants would rather go to see and hear Jolie.[21]

In some instances, celebrity participation at Davos made a leap from novelty to spontaneous drama. The best-known episode of this type occurred when Sharon Stone turned what would have been a high-level panel devoted to the question of how to fight malaria in Tanzania into a high-energy event involving audience involvement. Jumping up out of the crowd, the star of *Basic Instinct* and other movies said to the somewhat startled Tanzanian president, Benjamin Mkapa: "I'd like to offer you $10,000 to buy some bed nets today." Stone then called on the even more startled members of the audience to get out their checkbooks and deliver: "Just stand up. Just stand up. People are dying in his country today, and that is not OK with me." Through such theatrical behavior (complete with an atmosphere of a revivalist meeting, applause, and many reviews), Stone in her five minutes of Davos fame managed to get thirty executives to collectively raise $1 million.[22]

Beyond the freshness of spirit came the emotional lure of connecting a face and a character with salient issues. It played to another one of Davos's great strengths, in that as a site, it had long been personality- rather than company-driven. Klaus Schwab set the tone. But it was reinforced by the close connection of Davos with Bill Clinton, as well as such business celebrities as Bill Gates and George Soros.

Indeed, this cult of star personality emphasized the overwhelming sense of buzz vis-à-vis the entry of celebrity diplomats into the Davos scene. One reporter declared that the stodgy forum comes to life when "glitter meets gold. When a herd of cameramen approached, no one asked which leader or CEO was arriving, but which movie star had appeared, and what cause he or she was promoting."[23] The reporter who had compared the reception given to Jolie with that for the EU Commission president made a similar point by gushing, if in over-the-top fashion, "Look, there's Angelina Jolie! Angelina, how is the world faring on the health and human rights fronts? Oh, my gosh! It's Bono! Bono, what needs to be done about African poverty? Hey, Richard Gere and Sharon Stone, how can we tackle the AIDS crisis?"[24]

The mention of Bono points out the key connection between the different types of celebrities on full display at Davos. Bono was far more than just another of the established individuals within the growing cohort of celebrity diplomats. In terms of intensity Bono had few rivals, even when the entire ambit of Davos participants is included. In 2005, Bono appeared with what became known as the Davos "supergroup" comprising Bill Clinton, Tony Blair, Bill Gates, and Presidents Thabo Mbeki of South Africa and Olusegun Obasanjo of Nigeria. And the next day he was back on stage participating in another high-profile panel that included Gordon Brown and the Senegalese musician and activist Youssou N'Dour.

But it was not simply Bono's presence that lit up Davos. The essence of Bono's participation is how he deployed his voice across such a continuum of modalities. As elsewhere, Bono had a light but often biting touch. He could poke fun at the formal style of dress of the politicians in attendance at the forum, telling Gordon Brown that he might be "the last person wearing a suit at Davos."[25] But at the core of his mode of communication with either political leaders or corporate executives was the demand that the powerful deliver on their promises. His most telling comment during the supergroup session, of direct relevance to Blair and Gates, was this: "Our generation wants to be remembered for more than the Internet and the War on Terrorism." When Blair joked that mixing with the rich set at Davos made him wonder if he had made the right career choice, Bono retorted—with a mind to the upcoming Gleneagles summit—that this would be the year that "we would find out."[26]

Beyond words, Bono served as a major link with social change agents within the business community. Extending the principles of corporate social responsibility into targeted niche activities, Bono used Davos as the launching pad for his most ambitious operation of this type, the Product Red brand initiative. Surrounded by senior executives from a number of billion-dollar companies—American Express, the Gap, Giorgio Armani, and Converse/Nike (with Motorola added later)—Bono hitched his star to the cause of conscious consumerism via a scheme in which branded products would not just be made and imported from the South (such as a red T-shirt from the Gap made in Lesotho) but a share of the proceeds would be donated back for goals such as the elimination of HIV/AIDS in Africa. Although accepting that such an initiative would entail risks (including maintaining his own credibility), Bono cast this plan as the wave of the future, not the discredited past: "Philanthropy is like hippie music, holding hands. Red is more like punk rock, hip hop: this should feel like hard commerce. People see a world out of whack. They see the greatest health crisis in 600 years and they want to do the right thing, but they're not sure what that is. Red is about doing what you enjoy and doing good at the same time."[27]

Bono's hub network extends beyond the world of entertainment to a special relationship he has built with the two leading celebrity diplomats from the corporate world, Bill Gates and George Soros. Bono served as inspiration for some of the diplomatic activities embarked on by these corporate titans, a role Gates in particular has acknowledged. But Gates and Soros in turn provide substantial material backing for Bono's work through DATA. It received a number of grants, ranging from $250,000 to $500,000 for general operating costs from the Bill and Melinda Gates Foundation, with a larger sum in the amount of $2,250,000 awarded in 2003 for a three-year program to support debt relief and education about AIDS in Africa.[28] For its part, George Soros's flagship operation, the Open Society Institute (OSI), has chipped in regular amounts of $500,000 for general operating costs.

Although very different in their backgrounds and in some areas of policy orientation, these different types of celebrities have taken on a closely entangled set of activities. The buzz generated by Bono—operating on the premise that "Your first responsibility is not to be dull"—has been wedded to the bite that enormous wealth allows.[29] The connection is expressed at the declaratory level. Melinda Gates has referred to the "joint cause" between Bono and the Gates Foundation.[30] Soros stated that Bono "represents a constituency that needs to be catered to."[31] However, it is also projected through elaborate links at the operational level. The Bill and Melinda Gates Foundation and George Soros's OSI were not just DATA's "founding partners": their involvement with the organization continues with their representation on DATA's board of directors. Consultants have also been known to move seamlessly between the organizations. In another indication of how interconnected this relationship is, the U2 album *How to Dismantle an Atomic Bomb* includes Bill and Melinda Gates and George Soros in the list of acknowledgments.

The Bite of Material Wealth

Many corporate executives—and, for that matter, individual business entrepreneurs—engage in high-stakes commercial diplomacy. Almost all of these activities are of a highly instrumental nature: the maximization of profit. To give just one illustration, Hank Paulson, the Goldman Sachs chief executive turned U.S. treasury secretary, visited China alone some seventy times over a fifteen-year period for investment banking purposes.[32]

By this criterion, what are we supposed to make of Bill Gates and George Soros stretching out the contours of their activities? Both enjoy formidable reputations as hardheaded businessmen. As giant players in their respective areas of enterprise—Gates in high-tech via Microsoft (by 2000 the largest company in the world by market capitalization) and Soros in financial and currency transactions through his original Quantum Fund or, subsequently, the Soros Management Fund—they accumulated massive material resources and an attendant cult of celebrity. Neither dropped their main games from their Davos repertoire. Gates continued to speak on topics related to the future of technology, and Soros provided an annual assessment of currency markets.

Where Gates and Soros differed from most of their corporate counterparts at Davos was in the manner in which their embrace of diplomatic techniques took shape. Moving beyond the traditional deal-making business style associated with Davos, Gates and Soros became principal agents of celebrity diplomacy.

Temperamentally, neither Gates nor Soros can be considered ideal candidates for this shift in identity as actors. They could be admired for their high-stakes risk taking, but they were both feared for their rapacious commercial practices as well. Gates has been constantly critiqued throughout his business career as an evil monopolist, charges given added credence by the antitrust actions brought against Microsoft not only by the U.S. government but also by the EU. As the quintessential commercial "Davos man," any recognition (never mind endorsement) of Gates as a celebrity diplomat had to contend with the conventional and contradictory image that his "presence on the world stage is symptomatic of the new hegemony of global brands, which enjoy … power unmatched by politicians."[33]

Gates reinforced these oversized personality traits even as he rebranded himself as a celebrity diplomat. Davos had to contend with Gates making demands to be on the program both as technological guru and as a supercharged activist on global social and economic issues. As a very frustrated Managing Director commented in the media in the context of Gates's demand in 2005 that he wanted to be on another panel with Bill Clinton, "I've already scheduled two major sessions for Bill Gates, and … that's it … he seems to want more and more."[34]

Soros had an even more tainted reputation.[35] A cunning speculator, he remained best known as the currency trader who had "broken" the Bank of England and gained $1 billion in the process, by forcing the UK out of the European Exchange Rate Mechanism on what became known as "Black Wednesday" (September 16, 1992). Following the Asian financial crisis five years later, the long-serving Malaysian prime minister, Mahathir Mohamad, was an especially harsh critic, accusing Soros of wanting to cause another financial shockwave in the region.[36]

Further, Soros's attachment to controversy was not limited to the financial world. He had a confrontational relationship with a wide number of leaders around the world, a group that included President Vladimir Putin of Russia and President Islam Karimov of Uzbekistan. Both were considered by Soros to be enemies of his ideal of "the open society." His highly visible and well-resourced opposition to President George W. Bush polarized opinion about him in the United States. To sympathizers in MoveOn.org and other anti-Bush groups, he was a champion of resistance not only to the war in Iraq but to an incipient authoritarian state at home. To his detractors, he was portrayed as a dangerous maverick: full of material resources, but with no sense of responsibility.

If more inclined by disposition to be placed in the antidiplomat category, both Gates and Soros reflect in exaggerated form the general shift by the commercial Davos elite to the role of celebrity diplomats. This move comes through far more explicitly in Soros's voice and attitude on global issues. By instinct, Soros remained a firm supporter of a new form of multilateralism. Unlike the hyper-globalists in the business community, he sought to bring fundamental reform to the core institutions at the center of the international order: the international financial institutions and the World Trade Organization (WTO). Equally, unlike the ultranationalists (or neoconservatives) so formidable in the U.S. debate, he preferred diplomatic solutions to those attempted and/or imposed by coercive means. The retired commander of the North Atlantic Treaty Organization (NATO) and Democratic presidential hopeful, General Wesley Clark, described this aspect of Soros's ethos in bold strokes: "He understands that it's diplomacy first. It's building common bridges and common interests between people and cultures that makes the world safe and that makes it prosperous for all of us, not conquering territory at the point of a bayonet. That's the last resort when everything else has failed."[37]

Gates shared Soros's distaste for unilaterally imposed state-centric solutions. He was a sharp critic, for instance, of the tightening of the U.S. visa restrictions in the post-9/11 environment. His preference continued to be for a thickening of globalism, with a diffusion of responsibilities in the management of international public policy. A good international citizenship approach by national governments was still taken to be important if this networked approach on display at Davos was to find traction. And in pursuit of this model, he put a premium on the United States becoming as generous in its global responsibilities as "countries like Norway, Denmark, Sweden and the Netherlands."[38] However, Gates was equally adamant that governments alone could not solve what he identifies as the problems of primary importance: those related to health (both generally and in regard to the eradication of pandemic diseases such as HIV/AIDS, malaria, and tuberculosis). His main message was that "companies needed to get this on their agenda" in order to combat "a real market failure … a failure of visibility, a failure of incentives, a failure of cooperation that has led to a very disastrous situation."[39]

Despite marked contrasts in their backgrounds, with Gates a product of a comfortable mainstream Seattle upbringing and Soros a Jewish Hungarian double refugee from Nazi and communist occupations, they share some fundamental characteristics as celebrity diplomats. Both bring a formidable degree of intensity—or even velocity—to their engagement with public policy issues. Soros was quick to respond on a global basis to any issue of interest to him, with particular reference to the cultural advance toward open societies in states transitioning from authoritarian to democratic regimes. Gates simply turned his bulldozer instincts and an obsession with "winning" from the commercial to the health arena. As one journalistic profile highlighted this thrust of his character: "The way [Gates] talked about wiping out malaria was how he used to talk about wiping out Netscape."[40]

Another mark of similarity was in the shape of their motivation. If their embrace of a social diplomatic purpose paralleled the initiative launched through the UN's corporate social responsibility campaign, the activities taken on by Gates and Soros maintained an autonomous edge. They had no wish to be involved in any cause that smacked of froth. What they wanted were the results that, to their immense frustration, did not seem to be produced through conventional routes, whether national or supranational. Both conveyed a distinctive form of emotional instrumentalism. As Bono characterized this problem-solving attitude on the part of Gates: "This isn't about compassion…. Bill Gates is not into nice sentimental efforts or whimsical support of hopeless causes. When Bill walks into the room, we are not expecting a nice warm fuzzy feeling."[41]

This competitive spirit spilled over into the relationship between Soros and Gates. In September 2006, Soros departed from his typical script of democracy-building programs, pledging $50 million to the Jeffrey Sachs–led Millennium Promise, the aim of which was to help eradicate extreme poverty in Africa. Soros still made it clear that he considered his own core agenda of democracy promotion to be of a much higher magnitude of operational sensitivity. At the 2007 WEF, Soros stated that although public health programs were important, they were "like apple pie" in that a consensus existed concerning their value.[42]

When either Soros or Gates talked at Davos, the other participants listened. But unlike Bono and the celebrity diplomats from Hollywood, this power of attraction was not based on a buzz derived from glamour or an engaging voice. What celebrity Soros and Gates enjoyed came from the bite attached directly to their material wealth. Soros's deep pockets can be seen in the global reach of OSI and his wider network of foundations, which operate in some fifty countries with annual budgets between $400 and $500 million. On individual projects designed to build and embed democratic regimes within open, tolerant, and self-critical societies, his resources more often than not surpassed those brought to bear by the traditional dominant actor in democracy promotion: the United States. In the two years leading up to the so-called Orange Revolution in Ukraine in 2004, the United States targeted about $58 million on Ukraine. Soros, through his International Renaissance Foundation, spent millions more to allow for a change in government through a fair electoral process, topped up by a promise made at Davos of other resources to consolidate democracy in Ukraine.[43]

The donations promised by Gates toward global health programs, which have often been made public in announcements at Davos, were in keeping with the extraordinary material resources (rising to some $34 billion by 2006) of the Bill and Melinda Gates Foundation. Some perspective on these dimensions can be captured when it is considered that the yearly dispensation of grants by this private foundation (some $1.4 billion) exceeds the annual budget of the World Health Organization.

From the time the foundation was established in 2000 (when Gates stepped down as CEO to become chair and chief software architect of Microsoft), Gates's sense of emotional embrace grew, sentiments that can be grasped by the type of language he began using in the public sphere: "I refuse to sit here and say, O.K. next problem, this one doesn't bother me. It does bother me. Very much. And the only way for that to change is to stop malaria. So that is what we are going to have to do."[44]

Those emotions translated easily into a series of enormous financial commitments that reflected the approach of his foundation. At Davos in 2001, the Gates Foundation pledged $100 million to the International AIDS Vaccine Initiative. In 2005 in the same venue, the Gates Foundation—in tune with the ethos of "saving lives now"—provided $750 million for targeting child immunization programs such as the GAVI Alliance (formerly known as the UN Global Alliance for Vaccines and Immunization).[45] At the 2006 WEF, Gates announced that he would triple his donation to $900 million for the Global Plan to Stop Tuberculosis.

It is tempting, as in the case of Bono, to inflate the transformative role played by Soros and Gates as celebrity diplomats. One biographer went so far as to endorse the view that Soros was the only private citizen in the world "with his own foreign policy" and the means to "implement it."[46] Media stories cast him as the chief agent for bringing about not only the Orange Revolution in Ukraine but also the peaceful overthrow in Georgia of Eduard Shevardnadze's government through the so-called Rose Revolution in 2003.

A more nuanced portrayal sees them less as architects of any master plan and more as entrepreneurs who use material resources to build networks of influence to facilitate delivery in issue-specific areas. As with Bono, this pattern of activity has a distinctive top-down quality. Gates drew close to a number of influential politicians in the course of the resiting of Davos and his own rebranding, including Gordon Brown, with whom he teamed up for a well-publicized "war on TB."[47] Soros, in a similar vein, supported Brown's proposals for shaking up the global financial architecture.

Yet, the horizontal as well as vertical contours of this type of activity must be noted as well. Notwithstanding the Gates Foundation's pivotal position in terms of resources, it remained on some issues at least as much a follower as a leader. Its push on immunization for neglected diseases, for example, mirrored closely the approach initiated by Médecins Sans Frontières. If Soros's voice could be used as a blunt instrument, his material resources were usually deployed in an indirect manner: going around traditional channels of official interaction with funds directed via societal actors across national boundaries. As his longtime friend Mark Malloch Brown—the former administrator of the UNDP and former deputy secretary-general to Kofi Annan—put it: "Soros has helped launch nongovernmental organizations that challenge … governments and spoken out against leaders whose policies, he maintained, harmed citizens."[48]

As in the dominant commercial sides of their lives, Gates and Soros have faced fierce criticism for their intrusive behavior. Detractors of Gates—and there have been many—challenged both his motivations and his mechanisms. His conversion away from the orthodox neoliberal Davos model was portrayed as either a ploy to gain tax benefits via the establishment of his foundation and/or a device to soften his "take-no-prisoners, hyper-competitive" image in the Rockefeller/Carnegie tradition before him.[49] His model of operation was viewed as flawed in a number of ways. It favored a research design that placed the onus on early-stage science, developing vaccines and drugs instead of relying on existing medicines and technology proven to be useful on the front lines of delivery to those in need.[50] It privileged a model of partnerships under conditions where the Gates Foundation held the advantage in terms of financial backing. As one critical study illustrates, "The Gates Foundation, as a 'majority shareholder' of the GAVI Fund, virtually maintains a veto right on all important decision making, which is further consolidated by its position as a permanent Alliance Board member."[51]

The negative judgments of Soros had at least as much sting and were far more varied in their origins. Autocrats under threat from the transnational networked approach countered that it was a strategy intended to bring into power actors loyal to Soros. Unfortunately, some of his more creative proposals, such as the joint venture with UNDP to split the cost of salaries for a wide variety of state officials within the new government of President Mikheil Saakashvili in Georgia, reinforced this impression. Intended to provide salaries that would be sufficient to deter bribes, the plan signaled to many critical observers that the government was being "paid by Soros." Left-wing critics joined in this chorus, instinctively suspicious that a currency speculator could be promoting innovations in governance: "George Soros: The billionaire trader has become eastern Europe's uncrowned king and the prophet of 'the open society.' But open to what?"[52]

Still, valuable compensation for both Gates and Soros came in the form of diplomatic access and recognition that spread well beyond the Davos site. Although it is too far-fetched to say that Soros is a global statesman with an all-encompassing approach, his bite lent him enormous profile and, at least in some areas, clout. Some appreciation of this celebrity presence is garnered in Malloch Brown's somewhat offhand remark: that he would be hard-pressed to think of a "nongovernmental figure in the U.S. today—except perhaps Oprah ... who has as much power or influence overseas ... as does Soros."[53]

Bill Gates, or more accurately, Bill and Melinda Gates (as Melinda Gates has had far more time to look after the day-to-day running of the foundation) shared with Soros a huge amount of access to policy players around the world.[54] The only difference came in their treatment as diplomatic actors. Upping the ante on even Soros, some of the Gates's tours of health programs sponsored by the foundation took on the character of state visits. One trip to Bangladesh, profiled in the *Financial Times*, featured a ten-car entourage, complete with a military escort and an ambulance, as well as roadblocks and snipers.[55] Another to Vietnam in April 2007 included a meeting with Prime Minister Nguyen Tan Dung (a leader who had made his initial appearance at the WEF at the beginning of the same year), as well as representatives from the WHO, UNICEF, and nonprofit organizations.

THE FUTURE OF DAVOS

To illuminate the theatrical elements of Davos—in which the World Economic Forum and its key participants have gone through a process of resiting—is not to minimize the challenges to its run as the central hub of a transformed diplomacy. A number of threats to the dominant position of Davos come from both outside and inside its established structure. All have some potential to loosen the grip of Davos as the annual business-oriented event to be seen at and to participate in.

One challenge to Davos comes from nationalist state officials who celebrate power over diplomacy. The shift from the Clinton administration to the Bush administration—the substitution of what has been called "Crawford man" for Davos man—downgraded the event for Washington, D.C., insiders.[56] The few U.S. officials who attended in Bush's first term did so with little enthusiasm or impact.

As the fortunes of the Bush administration have waned, however, the stature of Davos has rebounded. Restrictive forms of coalitions of the willing are discredited, together with the closed framework of distinguishing "us" and "them." In order to mediate this form of deep division, Davos and some general engagement with celebrity diplomacy became more important. Condoleezza Rice has begun to engage positively with Bono and other key Davos actors in an extension of the diverse connections that distinguishes this new form of networked diplomacy.

A second challenge to Davos comes from below, in the form of the World Social Forum (WSF) and other civil society-driven expressions of anti-Davos sentiment. The WSF aims to hit the WEF where it hurts, with attacks on its legitimacy as a representative site for diplomacy. These attacks have posed some discomfort for those associated with the Davos model, as witnessed by the mix of responses to this challenge. One approach has been to invite high-profile WSF celebrities, such as Walden Bello, to the WEF. Another has been to try to build channels of communication and mediation between Davos and the WSF. President Luiz Inácio Lula da Silva of Brazil physically straddled the line between the two events, in that he made the effort to attend both the WSF (held in Porto Alegre, in southern Brazil) and the rival WEF in 2003. And in keeping with his hybrid role as a member of the business elite and an international reformer, George Soros served as one agent of dialogue between the two sites through the medium of a satellite hookup.

These facilitative (or harmonizing) devices resulted in mixed outcomes. Lula drew rave reviews, whereas Bello used his invitation to Davos to sharpen his attacks on the forum, declaring that "it would be good for the thousands of businessmen in Davos to be loaded into a space ship and for that space ship to take off."[57] And Soros was drowned out by a myriad set of voices of protest. A deeply disillusioned Soros did not repeat this experience, declaring that there were boundaries to his willingness to engage in this type of dialogue: "my masochism has it limits."[58]

However, even if the WSF continues to inflict some damage on the reputation of Davos, in other ways it embellishes its presence as a site for diplomatic interaction. All publicity is good publicity, especially when the culture of celebrity has been reproduced to some extent at the WSF. Started as a grassroots event, the WSF has morphed into a site in which the celebrities of the counterconsensus are showcased. In one of the many debates concerning the future of the WSF, at least one eminent public intellectual argued that there should be more transparency concerning not only the site of the event, and who could or could not be excluded from attendance, but significantly "who will speak at the plenary sessions (the 'stars')."[59]

Another set of challenges comes from within the Davos community. On the one hand, some signs of defection are evident with the launch of the Clinton Global Initiative (CGI). Turning on Davos as a talk shop ("I'm learning all this stuff but nobody ever asked me to do anything"), Clinton has located his own event, initially held in New York in September 2005, as a site for action.[60] As with the outsider challenge from the WSF, this insider critique, that Davos is little more than attractive window dressing, merits serious appraisal. As witnessed by a variety of actions it took in response to the 2004 Indian Ocean tsunami (with Davos partners joining forces to manage the emergency distribution of aid through Colombo airport in Sri Lanka), the WEF has not completely sat on the sidelines. The prime function of Davos, ultimately, is to serve as a galvanizer for action, not as a platform for collective endeavors.

The inevitable question that hangs over the CGI is whether it will complement or compete with Davos. If the former, a delicate truce can be maintained allowing the two events to coexist. Through 2006, this scenario appeared to move out in front. Despite his criticism, Clinton maintained his image as the quintessential Davos man at the 2006 WEF, and the two meetings had a good deal of overlapping membership.[61] In 2007, however, Clinton was a notable absentee from Davos as the CGI prepared for a mid-year meeting in New York City in April. If that was a sign of widening split, some mounting tensions were inevitable. Competition had already surfaced in terms of attendance and showcasing initiatives. Whereas Davos had been the prime site for announcements by Bill Gates on health issues, the CGI has begun to be the forum of choice for other business celebrities. A notable case in point was the pledge by Sir Richard Branson of a multibillion-dollar investment on global warming at the September 2006 CGI.[62]

The final challenge comes from an urge by some at Davos to go back to basics. The direction adopted by Soros and Gates—and the resiting of Davos more generally—has not and never will be to the taste of some within the business community. Their argument is that issues of corporate social responsibility stretch the boundaries beyond what should be the essence of Davos: getting the fundamentals right. One critic suggested a solution: "business leaders should boycott these pointless gatherings—and their shareholders should hold them to account for wasting everyone's time and money if they continue to attend."[63] Another targeted the cause: "Davos has become so celebrity-obsessed it can no longer manage serious debate on the issues that matter in business."[64]

That final challenge would appear to have the greatest capacity to derail Davos. Fatigue is a factor here, as the celebrity diplomats (in the entertainment if not the business world) might simply wear out their welcome. Or alternatively, new economic conditions will refocus their attention away from ethical concerns. As it is, new stars are beginning to be found in the emergent markets of China and India.

Both trends appeared to be buttressed by the 2007 Davos guest list. India and China continued to supply much of the new buzz, with business entrepreneurs such as Sunil Mittal (the CEO of the giant Bharti telecom and retail group in India) rising as new stars at the event. Hollywood celebrities, by way of contrast, were noticeable not only for their absence but by the manner by which this omission was explained. As Klaus Schwab put it bluntly: "We noticed that there was undue publicity given to the attendance of those celebrities at the last meeting. We have to be careful that we are not hijacked by the celebrity world."[65]

The strongest brake to be applied to this shift in emphasis is that the different layers of celebrity culture have become completely embedded at Davos. Without this type of imparted buzz—or without a different bite—Davos risks losing its pivotal position. The value of Davos has in large part become its theatrical or "cabaret" nature, with tremendous doses of drama and personality.[66]

Even a temporary "time out" on the presence of stars at the Davos in 2007 was met with misgivings, with Schwab himself acknowledging the risk that fewer celebrities would mean less media coverage.[67] Moreover, the exclusion of Hollywood personalities did not mean a total ban. The absence of glamorous enthusiasts such as Angelina Jolie did not extend to other categories of celebrity diplomats. Bono, Bill Gates, and George Soros were very much on the scene.

Above all, Davos showcases the ongoing struggle between images of decline and adaptation in diplomacy and diplomatic sites. One of the age-old problems of diplomacy is an inability to stir emotions in the way that other public activities can. Davos has found a formula that contradicts this image.

By embracing celebrities, Davos has embraced as well the celebration of diplomacy. Its deficiency, as with celebrity diplomacy as a whole, lies within its limited ambit. Davos has jacked up the intensity, the form, and the scope of diplomacy, but it is still a site that is restrictive in its claim to territorial membership. The vulnerability of Davos—or celebrity diplomacy—is its concentration in the North. It is this gap that needs scrutiny before any full treatment of celebrity diplomacy can be deemed complete.

☆ 6 ☆

(Uneasily) Moving Celebrity Diplomacy beyond the Anglo-Sphere

The image of celebrity diplomacy presented so far contains a striking disjunction. The ultimate objective behind this cosmopolitan activity is to further the oneness of humanity. A universal ethos is presented that is very much at odds with parochial attitudes and the tight restrictions of sovereignty. National (and self) interests are played down, while a sense of global citizenship is emphasized.[1] The idea is, to paraphrase Bono's words from the U2 song "One": "We've got to carry each other."[2]

In terms of its agency, however, what stands out about the expression of celebrity diplomacy is its restrictiveness. The actors at the core of the enterprise are not just a small group located in the northwestern quadrant of the globe. They belong to a narrow subset of extremely high-profile individuals whose fame is a projection of the cultural power of the Anglo-sphere, whether based in Hollywood or the metropolitan axes of the music industry. Celebrity diplomats may emerge from different fragments of this empire and speak with a range of accents, but they do so in the confines of an English-speaking orbit, with its two central hubs across the Atlantic in the United States and the United Kingdom. Ownership of this project is narrowly constructed, with trespassing by outsiders carefully controlled.

The causal dynamics behind this web of domination are in large part structural. All of the major celebrities profiled in this book are enveloped in an elaborate form of machinery—involving public relations firms, brand

91

consultants, and studios. A symbiosis of interests exists between the individual and this multilayered industry, which tries to squeeze every bit of publicity out of any and all of their activities. By way of contrast, there is little or no incentive to look beyond the geographic confines of this industry. The manufacture and projection of celebrities—like the wider process of globalization—is a top-down process radiating out of the Anglo-sphere. There is no reciprocal movement from below, with stars from the South given equitable space in the celebrity structure.

More difficult to assess is the role of the celebrity diplomats profiled in this book as accomplices in this regulatory process. In some cases, celebrity diplomats have taken on an explicit disciplinary function in determining which performers and issues get exposure and which do not. Bob Geldof's controversial selection process in the Live 8 concerts brought this issue to a head, as he was accused of reproducing a system of "musical apartheid" in his bias toward featuring older white "gods" of rock over African stars in the concerts under his command.[3] Does that represent an anomalous situation? Bono's mentorship role among a diverse but exceptional group of entertainers from both inside and outside the Anglo-sphere contradicts this image. So does the interest that other celebrity diplomats, most notably Angelina Jolie, have taken in the celebration of culture from Africa as part of their global reach. Yet, even as we are mindful of this extended sense of appreciation, we see that structure appears to trump agency in this arena as well. The advisory group for both Bono and Jolie remains Anglo-sphere-centric. And as illustrated by the organizational structure of DATA, this bias is a central feature of the pivotal organization that binds the network of celebrity diplomats from Bono to the Bill and Melinda Gates Foundation and George Soros's Open Society Institute. Significantly, not one member of DATA's board of directors comes from outside the Anglo-sphere.[4]

The effect of this restrictiveness plays out in the non Anglo-sphere in an uneven fashion. Within the continental European countries, especially France, there has been a pronounced parting of ways between their celebrity culture and that found in the Anglo-sphere. Celebrity diplomacy as profiled throughout this book has found little resonance in these cultures. The framework of UN goodwill ambassadors has not found much buy-in, and freelance activity has continued to take very different shapes.

The African response has been far more animated. With Africa as the focus of so much of the activity of celebrity diplomats, there was anticipation that Africans themselves would become an integral part of the dynamics of celebrity diplomacy. Yet they found themselves to be excluded on a number of counts. At the cultural level, the expectation that African entertainers would be able to use the dynamic to reach a massive global audience was frustrated—a marginalization brought to the fore at Live 8. The concert in Hyde Park might be the central site of a new form of societal mobilization about Africa. But African entertainers remained on the sidelines. The corollary was that few African entertainers were acknowledged as celebrity diplomats. The supply was available for a leap of this sort, both through established artists such as the great Senegalese musician Youssou N'Dour and a rising cluster of other attractive and sophisticated stars. But the demand for full northern exposure was held in tight check.

This sense of omission, although not a project breaker on the days of its most publicized events, has the potential to drain much of the goodwill of celebrity diplomacy on an ongoing basis. The efficiency as well as the legitimacy of the enterprise will be called into question if its representative boundaries are not expanded to encompass the global South. Bono, Geldof, Angelina Jolie, and the other best-known celebrity diplomats may know something about Africa, but any attempt to portray themselves as experts with respect to the continent will come across as paternalism or as an expression of benign neocolonialism. Just as the motivations of the celebrity diplomats are increasingly scrutinized in the North, so too is there intense reflection about the pros and cons of this form of activity in the South. It is especially true among Africans, who have in their midst many individuals who possess the potential to be valuable assets in this type of activity.

BETWEEN PUBLIC INTELLECTUALS AND ECCENTRIC INDIVIDUALISM IN EUROPE

The domination by the Anglo-sphere in the creation and spread of celebrity diplomacy is not simply an issue for the developing world. It is a global phenomenon that has an impact in the non-Anglo-sphere domain of the North as well as the South. The distinction has a strong attachment to levels of confidence at the societal level. In continental Europe, being outside the domain of the Anglo-sphere has been seen by many public intellectuals as a source of cultural strength. And their role has been defined according to well-rehearsed scripts on how to cultivate celebrity status. The avoidance of the more flexible approach from the Anglo-sphere is as much by choice as an inability to follow this model.

On the major strands of celebrity diplomacy, continental Europe has lagged behind the Anglo-sphere leadership. This scarcity of attention comes out strongly in terms of the low profile that Europeans have adopted in respect to the position of UN goodwill ambassador. The United States in particular has become saturated with accomplished personnel (albeit across a wide spectrum of expertise), including a range of messengers of peace who encompass not only Michael Douglas but Elie Wiesel, Muhammad Ali, Wynton Marsalis, Magic Johnson, and Marian Wright Edelman.

Continental Europeans, by way of comparison, have demonstrated little enthusiasm for this form of engagement. The monumental exception has been Luciano Pavarotti, the celebrated opera singer who has not only acted as a UN messenger of peace but also was a UNICEF ambassador. This exceptionalism is in close conformity with Pavarotti's boundary-straddling role in other components of his public life. For one thing, he was one of the rare classical entertainers able to become a mainstream star. Not only was his 1990 recording *Nessun Dorma* a breakthrough hit in the UK market, his performances as one of the "Three Tenors" rivaled rock as a medium for popular spectacles.

For another thing, Pavarotti had become as well networked as any of the celebrity diplomats positioned in the Anglo-sphere. One measure of this network power was his close connection in the 1990s with two of the biggest stars in this arena through his participation in an initiative designed to aid child victims in war-torn Bosnia. Princess Diana visited Pavarotti in Verona in support of a concert he hosted in September 1993 as a fundraiser. Pavarotti consolidated a long working partnership with Bono, who had also become obsessed with the Bosnian conflict (linking Sarajevo by satellite to European venues of the Zooropa tour). One major event of this partnership was the staging of a huge peace concert in 1997 (two years after the Dayton Peace Accords) in which Pavarotti teamed up with Bono to sing "Miss Sarajevo." Another was their joint activity to help establish a musical therapy center for children of all ethnic backgrounds in Mostar, one of the cities most devastated by the fighting in Bosnia.

Pavarotti's style in his UN-related activities owed far more to Danny Kaye and Peter Ustinov than Angelina Jolie and other recent ambassadors. He was extremely energetic in his engagements, devoting himself generously to "Pavarotti and Friends" concerts for Afghanistan refugees in Pakistan (2001), Angolan refugees in Zambia (2002), and Iraqi refugees in Iran (2003). In addition he offered to screen UN public service announcements and promotional videos during his worldwide farewell tour of forty concerts in 2005–2006.

Unfortunately, due to no fault of his own, Pavarotti's activities caused controversy. The partner organization he worked with in establishing the musical therapy center (to be named the Pavarotti Musical Center) became bogged down in allegations of mismanagement and corruption. And

Pavarotti—along with many other patrons of the project—chose to walk away from the project to avoid embarrassment.[5]

The other two UN messengers of peace from Europe highlight the distinctive nature of engagement in this process in other ways. The first of these individuals, Enrico Macias, shows the tensions in Europe between localism and cosmopolitanism. Unlike the majority of U.S. messengers of peace, Macias cannot be called a star with a global reach. Nonetheless, it is interesting to note that Macias has sold an enormous number of records (over 50 million) in the Francophone world dating back to the early 1960s.

Adding complexity to the situation is the hybrid image of Macias as an Algerian-born Jewish singer caught up in the apparently intractable controversies of the Middle East. Macias had built up his reputation on songs based on loss within the region, whether through physical displacement ("J'ai quitté mon pays") or violent ruptures ("Un Berger vient de tomber," on the assassination of Egyptian president Anwar Sadat). Still he could not escape accusations of partiality. After he appeared at a pro-Israel rally, protestors rallied at his concerts with banners denouncing him as "not an ambassador of peace, but an ambassador of Israel."[6] And notwithstanding an official invitation from President Abdelaziz Bouteflika for Macias to tour Algeria forty years after he had left, fears for his safety prevented him from making this return visit. Being a messenger of peace did not make him an intercivilizational warrior: "It's clear that going to [Algeria] is not like going to other places. There is not a zero risk. I am a singer, not Don Quixote or a hero."[7]

The second European messenger of peace is the Italian author and journalist Anna Cataldi. As a serious observer of war, her credentials are impeccable. Her best-known book is *Letters from Sarajevo*, on the experiences of youth in the Balkans war. But she has also collaborated on the ambitious project, *Crimes of War: What the Public Should Know*, with American journalists Roy Gutman and David Rieff.

With the striking anomaly of Elie Wiesel and arguably the children's rights activist Marian Wright Edelman, comparing Cataldi to the bulk of the U.S. messengers of peace is a case of very incompatible categorizations. What the UN is searching for in the United States are popular entertainers. By way of contrast, Cataldi is the classic European public intellectual. If the choice was between "glitter" and "gravitas," the United States stood at one end and Europe at the other end of the spectrum.[8]

Even if continental Europe was able to supply a very different quality and quantity of UN ambassadors, their global impact remains in doubt. Non-Anglo-sphere celebrities continued to find it difficult to attract the same level of publicity as their counterparts from the U.S./UK hubs. The Japanese experience illustrates the extent of this asymmetry. Japanese celebrities, unlike their European counterparts, formed an impressive cluster of UN goodwill ambassadors. Furthermore, this grouping did not fit the stereotypes of conformists. One impressive example is Misako Konno, an author, TV personality, and actress. As a UN messenger of peace, she was quite prepared to speak her mind on an array of international issues. Visiting Vietnam, she voiced her regret that Japan had not done a better job of preserving the traditional way of life. She added her opinion that the victims of "Agent Orange" she came across in Vietnam reminded her of Japanese victims of the atomic bombs. Expressing the view that she "was stunned by the disparity in living standards between Israelis and Palestinians" when visiting Gaza and the Palestinian autonomous areas in 2000, she urged the international community to continue financial support for the Palestinians.[9]

If less controversial, Tetsuko Kuroyanagi, another well-known writer of children's books (including the best-selling *Totto* series), TV personality, and traveler, was elevated to a high status through her role as a goodwill ambassador for UNICEF. Her moment in the global spotlight came when, with an array of UN peace envoys in attendance, she cut the ribbon with Michael Douglas for the new disarmament exhibition at UN headquarters in New York. With charred artifacts relocated from the atomic sites in Nagasaki and Hiroshima forming its centerpiece, this permanent display took up a prime location in the corridor outside the General Assembly Hall.

Even with a high level of commitment, this cohort of Japanese personalities fell short in the degree of global recognition that the standard-bearers from the Anglo-sphere received as celebrity ambassadors. It is hardly an exaggeration to say that Elton John attracted more publicity in the global press when he stated during 1998 that he was too busy to accept an invitation from Secretary-General Annan to help the UN programs against AIDS.

Nor, to embellish this argument further, is there any comparison in the journalistic coverage on an international basis between the activities of Konno and Kuroyanagi and the publicity generated by the appointment of Nicole Kidman as a UNIFEM goodwill ambassador in 2006. Kidman came from outside the U.S./UK part of the Anglo-sphere. And she had little inclination to be a magnet for controversy, shying away from any public statement concerning her beliefs on the issue of abortion.[10] Yet with her tremendous star power and the coincidence of life imitating art with her role in the UN-centered film *The Interpreter,* her appointment made a huge splash.

Europeans in the celebrity ranks have been equally detached from these networks, whether the tight variant associated with Bono through DATA or the looser version formed via the Make Poverty History campaign. DATA continued to run its European operations out of London through the Heiligendamm G8 process, and continental European celebrities appearing on the program at the Live 8 concerts in 2005 formed an eclectic mix. The event at Versailles, "Plus D'Excuses," included a number of high-profile presenters, including Juliette Binoche and Johnny Hallyday. But this participation appears to be one-time appearances with no follow-up in terms of networking. As in the case of Africa, Geldof's personal style left a poor aftertaste, and he was accused by German NGOs in particular of organizing the Live 8 concert in Berlin without consulting development groups.[11] The choice of entertainment reflected quite distinctive musical cultures. Die Toten Hosen, a German punk band whose song "Friss oder Stirb" (Eat or Die) was their biggest hit, took part in the Berlin event. Axelle Red, the self-styled queen of "French soul" music and UNICEF goodwill ambassador for Belgium, was included on the Versailles bill.

The only European celebrity who was able to speak to audiences in her home country (Germany) and throughout the Anglo-sphere was the supermodel Claudia Schiffer, who moved beyond the one-time involvement adopted by continental celebrities at the Live 8 events. She took part in a London "We'll Be Watching You" photo shoot organized by the Global Call to Action against Poverty. And she was one of the celebrity presenters at the concert outside Edinburgh on the day of the G8 summit.

Contradicting the image that she was in attendance to be seen and not heard, Schiffer sought to voice her concerns that the G8 leaders deliver on their promises. In a statement designed to push the embattled chancellor to do more to ratchet up the level of German ODA, she played the guilt card with a high level of emotionalism: "Gerhard Schröder, we are watching you. Since you woke up this morning, 30,000 have already died."[12]

Beyond the skepticism in the minds of at least some observers about any supermodel (a profession known for having a taste for excess!) pronouncing on poverty issues, Schiffer's own image was twisted and turned by her own global profile. Although German by upbringing, she epitomized the mainstream celebrity profile in that she lived and worked mainly in the hub countries of the Anglo-sphere. Unlike her Eurocentric counterparts, she had built up close and ongoing links with Bono and ONE: The Campaign to Make Poverty History, as well as larger social movements formed around the Gleneagles summit.

Uncomfortable with a model imported from the Anglo-sphere, Europeans favored the approach for the pursuit and projection of celebrity diplomacy stretched across the continuum from classic public intellectualism to

eccentric individualism. Running through both streams of behavior—epitomized by the French experience—has been a heavy dose of contrarianism.
Many of the most publicized forays of French public intellectuals have been
directed toward oppositional initiatives from the bottom up, such as those
associated with the WSF.

The extreme individualistic traits of French society are magnified by the
populist appeals emanating from mavericks with big axes to grind about
domestic and international issues. Standing out as an illustration of this tendency to brush uncomfortably against the world of celebrity diplomacy is the
eccentricity of Brigitte Bardot. Through one lens, the famous film star of the
1950s was simply another benign activist pursuing an extended campaign on
behalf of animal rights. Among her many other initiatives was a thirty-year war
against the seal hunt off the shores of Canada and Greenland.

Where Brigitte Bardot moved from benign to malevolent force was in
her stance on France's political and social identity. Flirting seriously with
the extreme right-wing party in French politics, the National Front, Bardot
decried the "Islamization" of France. Convicted in 1997 and 2000 of incit-
ing racial violence, and with an incendiary book (*Un Cri dans le silence*) to
her name, Bardot crossed the line of what was acceptable behavior for an
individual to be acknowledged as a celebrity diplomat.

Far harder to place on the continuum between public intellectual and eccentric individualist is Bernard Kouchner. As one of the prime originators of the
concept of "the duty to interfere," Kouchner's credentials as a public intellectual
ready and able to speak and write on the big issues of the day were impeccable.
Yet, if a thinker, Kouchner was also the quintessential man of action. At the
early stages of his career that dimension came to the fore in his "unofficial"
diplomatic work in establishing Médecins sans Frontières (MSF) in reaction
to the 1960s Biafra crisis. Later on, these categories were further scrambled as
Kouchner entered official life both in French domestic politics and at the UN.
In the former role, he served in socialist governments as both a minister for
social affairs with special responsibility for humanitarian aid and as a junior
health minister. In the latter role, he took on the arduous responsibility as the
chief UN administrator for Kosovo from 1999 to 2001.[13]

The nature of Kouchner's eccentricity is equally hard to pin down. His
love of media attention contributes to this image. Most of the narratives
characterize him as a publicity hound. His connection with MSF ended after
he chartered a hospital ship to rescue Vietnamese boat people in 1979, as
this initiative was deemed by the rest of this organization as an act of self-
promotion. He was ridiculed for trying to turn Operation Restore Hope in
Somalia into a long promotion for his own endeavors, as the cameras picked

him up wading ashore with sacks of rice. And as the de facto governor of Kosovo, he was accused of acting in an abrupt fashion with little concern for diplomatic protocol.

Standing back from this characterization, however, it is easy to see Kouchner not simply as an extreme individualist but as a figure ahead of his time in understanding the media. His public relations skills were world-class, but so was his ability to frame issues so that both state officials and the public would notice them. Underscoring his work was a blunt honesty about what needed to be done and why.

Because of this multidimensional public profile, Kouchner stands apart from the type of celebrity diplomat at the core of this book. He remains a huge celebrity in France and has remained popular despite taking unpopular stances (most notably, his approval of the U.S. invasion of Iraq).[14] He is also a figure who has constantly reconfigured his career across the unofficial/official divide, as seen again by his elevation in 2007 as foreign minister under the conservative government of Nicolas Sarkozy. This personal success, however, magnifies the difficulty with presenting Europeans in terms of the U.S./UK model. Continental exceptionalism, in celebrity diplomacy as in other matters, continues to live on.

AFRICA AS A SITE OF EXCLUSION OR INCUBATION FOR CELEBRITY DIPLOMATS

Africa's relationship with respect to celebrity diplomacy has been very different than Europe's. The place of European celebrities on the sidelines of this Anglo-centered enterprise has been one of detachment. With little enthusiasm to get involved, Europe remains only a minor and ill-fitting producer of celebrity diplomats. Neither is Europe the main arena where the sustained efforts of celebrity diplomats are channeled. A voluntary downplaying of this type of activity goes hand in hand with the low stakes concerning its application in the region.

Questions about how Africa has been dealt with as a subject and source of celebrity diplomacy and diplomats are far more controversial. Some debate has broken out about the manner in which hub celebrity diplomats have branded Africa. It would be wrong to suggest that the celebrity diplomats from the Anglo-sphere are "tragedy voyeurs" fascinated by Africa as a site of disaster and catastrophe. Bono has repeatedly commented on the beauty of Africa. Angelina Jolie has likewise showcased Africa as a continent full of potential.

Yet despite these bursts of declaratory enthusiasm, a chasm opened up between an operational appreciation of all these well-intended acts of goodwill and the central message about the condition of Africa. African celebrities, such as Youssou N'Dour, acknowledged that initiatives along the lines of Live 8 elevated the position of Africa, as deserving of justice and equity, on the world's mental map. What he and other entertainers were sensitive about was the image of hope and opportunity being subordinated to the commonplace habit of seeing Africa as one big collective basket case without geographical differentiation or an awareness that sites of both success and failure exist. N'Dour kept reiterating that celebrities such as Bob Geldof should "come to Africa more, to talk to people more, and hear our advice.... We don't want pity."[15]

The issue of ownership of the celebrity diplomat model was also acutely sensitive. An authentic African celebrity such as N'Dour expressed his desire to move into the first ranks of this enterprise, viewing it as "a chance to proclaim himself an ambassador for Africa, and to be able to represent it on the world stage."[16] A more inclusive approach to celebrity diplomacy, though, faced enormous obstacles.

As noted, the absence of recognition for African cultural diplomats does not mean that there is an absence of availability. At the crest of this constellation stands Nelson Mandela. After retiring from official office as president of the new postapartheid South Africa, Mandela continued to use his celebrity status in a quasi-official manner. His activity centered on his role as intermediary in a number of high-risk cases, including the brokerage of a deal to help end the standoff between Libya and western nations over the surrender of two Libyan agents charged in the 1988 Lockerbie bombing of Pan-Am Flight 103.

Freedom from governmental responsibilities also allowed Mandela to wedge out from his position as a political icon to become a global cultural celebrity. When in prison, Mandela had been the subject of a number of freedom concerts, including a massive one at Wembley Stadium to celebrate his seventieth birthday in 1988. In his postpolitical life, Mandela used similar mechanisms to help raise money for the Nelson Mandela Foundation. A November 2003 Cape Town concert (named after Mandela's prison number, 46664) in support of his work on AIDS/HIV brought together a fascinating mix of celebrities (most notably Bono and Geldof), along with bands from the hub Anglo-sphere countries and Africa.

With this context in mind, Mandela was the star that the Live 8 could not do without. In dramatic fashion he appeared on the giant screen at the back of the stage in the Murrayfield/Edinburgh concert for Live 8: The

Final Push. Introduced by Bono, Mandela provided a clarion call for action beyond the establishment: "Sometimes it falls upon a generation to be great. You can be that generation. You have that opportunity."[17]

The reputational credibility and power of mobilization possessed by Mandela had a tremendous upside. The downside was that his charismatic persona was so large that it put—or perhaps, more accurately, rationalized putting—other African celebrities on the sidelines. The patronage and presence of Mandela were seen as enough!

Certainly the disconnect between the place of honor accorded to Mandela and the exclusionary practices facing African entertainers during the Live 8 process is very striking. To call these practices "musical apartheid" has a harsh and exaggerated tone to it. Nonetheless, the extent of the inequity between the billing given to aging white rock stars from the Anglo-sphere hub and the neglectful treatment given to African stars stands out as a visible stain on the proceedings. Critics, both in oppositional circles in the United States and United Kingdom and within Africa, could use the slogan "Saving Africans without Africans" to effectively denigrate the entire celebrity/Live 8 project.[18]

As controversy swelled over the nonexposure of African performers, the excuse proffered by Bob Geldof, that in the rush to organize the Live 8 events he called the acts that he knew, does not cut it. As noted, Geldof was in Cape Town in 2003 at the Mandela concert at which a number of well-known African musicians—including Youssou N'Dour, Baaba Maal, and Angelique Kidjo—performed. All had the talent not only to share the stage with the group of rock stars that Geldof and his team assembled, but they also had the profile to serve as celebrity diplomats. All were artists who straddled the Francophone-Anglophone and North/South divides, on top of which they had extensive experience working with the UN as goodwill ambassadors.

What is more, the list of concessions granted to African performers revealed a sense of embarrassment concerning this deficiency, although they received neither an apology nor adequate recompense at the main events. One form of compensation came through the decision to add one more Live 8 concert (the only one outside a G8 country) in Johannesburg, South Africa. A second form of compensation was provided through the pulling together of the Eden Project's "Africa Calling," an event championed by Peter Gabriel and the World of Music, Arts, and Dance organization, featuring a number of African star performers at a site in the Biosphere in Cornwall. And a third form of compensation was offered via the upgrading of Youssou N'Dour's place at the Live 8 concerts. In a reprise of the role that Phil Collins had played in the original Live Aid concerts—traveling by helicopter, Concorde, and small plane between London and Philadelphia—N'Dour was flown by helicopter and plane between Hyde Park, the Eden Project, and the French concert in Versailles.

If these concessions were designed to soothe the impact of this revisionist program, they were more salt in the wounds that had been opened up by the controversy. The Johannesburg event had all the trappings of a last-minute event, with small crowds in an improvised setting. Africa Calling, although attracting big name performers (and some megastars from outside the music industry, most notably Angelina Jolie, who introduced some of the acts), was overshadowed by Hyde Park. It also suffered psychologically from the perception that the performers were the B-squad, out of step with Geldof's desire to pack the main events with the best-selling artists of the rock star world. As Peter Gabriel conceded, whether sarcastically or not: "We would have loved to have seen more African artists in Hyde Park. However, Bob's [Geldof] point of view is that the principal job of this event is to get billions of eyes all round the world to watch all the messages they have contained in this programme and any unfamiliar artist … may cause people to channel-switch. I don't agree but I am very happy we have Live 8's blessing and Bob's blessing."[19]

As alluded to earlier in this chapter, N'Dour's own reaction combined fascination and frustration. On the one side he was impressed and comforted that all the power behind Live 8 was intended to help Africa. But he was very uneasy about the manner in which African performers had been shut out (notwithstanding his inclusion in the Hyde Park program, he still performed with a non-African performer, Dido), as well as the images of suffering in Africa that were used to market the Live 8 concerts. From his perspective, the need was to look at Africa as a diverse continent with a rich tapestry of people and places, not as one large homogeneous and failed country.[20]

N'Dour deserved star billing. In terms of musical pedigree, he had broken out of the world music box to enter the mainstream market. A huge star in France, N'Dour had sung at the opening ceremony of the 1998 World Cup. His English-language pedigree was assured by his 1994 hit record in the UK (sung with Neneh Cherry), "7 Seconds."

Yet to accord N'Dour's status at Live 8 because of his musical credentials ignores his other public attributes. His potential as a global celebrity diplomat matched that of the galaxy of stars I have profiled in this book. His organization-oriented resume glittered in its scope and continuity. He had performed at concerts for the liberation of Nelson Mandela, for Amnesty International, for Jubilee 2000, and for victims of AIDS/HIV. He had also been a UNICEF goodwill ambassador since 1991 and, among other activities, took part in the United against Malaria campaign and the 2001 launching of UNICEF's Global Movement for Children.

Dating back to his appearance in 1985 at the original Live Aid concert, where he performed with a contingent of African musicians, his networking credentials were equally impressive. He had become a regular panel discussant at Davos and a close confidant of Bono. Indeed, he called himself Bono's "Africa correspondent."[21]

On top of these characteristics, N'Dour had the ideal personality for a celebrity diplomat. His serenity shone through all his activities. His music was far less politically charged than that of other stars, such as the late Nigerian band leader Fela Anikulapo-Kuti or Thomas Mapfumo (known as "Zimbabwe's musical ambassador to the world"). And religious tolerance is a central theme on his *Egypt* album, released amid heated talk about civilizational clashes in the post-9/11 environment.[22]

Calmness did not mean a lack of determination. On the policy issues on which he chose to concentrate, he proved a fierce advocate, as illustrated most vividly in his work on the campaign to stop the flow of dangerous waste material from North to South. His song "Toxic Waste" captures his cry of anger on this issue. N'Dour also showed that he was willing to sacrifice material success for points of principle. As a matter of conscience, he cancelled a major U.S. tour (with thirty-eight engagements) in protest of the U.S. invasion of Iraq.

N'Dour stands out among African musicians, but unlike Mandela he does not have the effect of being so big that other celebrities get lost. The struggle between the structural forces restricting the exposure of African stars in the entertainment world and the position of Africa as an incubator for creativity runs through a much larger spectrum. The examples of Angelique Kidjo and Baaba Maal showcase many of the dynamics found in this struggle. The sense of hurt or even insult concerning both the portrayal of Africa and their own neglect comes out in their assessment of the entire event.

Kidjo, a dynamic singer and songwriter from Benin who was placed on the alternative lineup at Eden Park, let her feelings be known in an interview with CNN International: "It's time that people in the Western world give the microphone to the African people to talk about their own problems. Every time you hear about Africa, it's always disaster."[23]

The criticism from Maal, a high-profile Senegalese musician whose achievements include a Grammy nomination, was directed toward the sustainability of the effort. It was one thing to engage in a number of concentrated activities targeting the condition of Africa. It was a completely different thing to make a difference on an ongoing basis. As he warned, getting results meant a long-term investment of ambitious proportion: "It's not just the one year that people are going to talk or make plans for Africa. It's going to be decades, and decades if they're really sincere to do what they're promising to do."[24]

As with N'Dour, both Kidjo and Maal spoke with a confidence that came not just from their position as prominent entertainers but from their high-profile public personalities as celebrity diplomats. Kidjo had devoted a good deal of her time to the issues of child trafficking and young people orphaned by HIV/AIDS in Africa. Maal's scope of activities was amazing by any standard. Fluent in English and French as well as several African languages, Maal was an experienced and passionate goodwill ambassador for UNDP on HIV/AIDS awareness and its efforts to help this genera-tion of AIDS orphans. His ability to balance the worlds of entertainment and public service ratcheted up over time, as he was invited to perform in special events such as the concert to celebrate Wangari Maathai's recep-tion of the Nobel Peace Prize. Watched by tens of millions of viewers at a show hosted by Tom Cruise and Oprah Winfrey, Maal sang the song "African Woman" to the Kenyan environmentalist who had moved into Bono's network.

Akin to N'Dour, Maal combined a philosophical bent with an activist spirit. Maal was equally at home giving a lecture on contemporary Afri-can society at the British Museum and collaborating with a wide range of artists at the launch of an event devoted to Africa at the massive Remi festival.

Above all else, Maal epitomized the ability of African celebrities to be-come hybrids with both an inside and outside dimension to their profile. Maal traveled to Gleneagles with antipoverty activists, but he also had impressive access to decision makers. One UK journalist described Maal's mode of operation as rivaling the access of the celebrity diplomat at the apex of the enterprise: "Like N'Dour, Baaba Maal has a lot of political clout. He has meetings with the World Bank, and ministers take his calls. The only Western equivalent might be Bono, who seems to be able to walk into the White House and demand reductions of Third World debt."[25]

STRUCTURAL IMPEDIMENTS FROM THE INSIDE

One key question left untouched by this discussion is how particular the African experience has been in terms of celebrity diplomacy. Africa has been on the front lines of the debates about the exposure of celebrity entertainers. The potential of celebrity diplomacy, never mind the rest of the global South, has not been fully realized. Detailing some other possibilities, even if limited to snapshot accounts, helps flesh out the opportunities and constraints of this enterprise from a bottom-up perspective.

One of the advantages enjoyed by at least some African countries in their supply of possible celebrity diplomats is governmental structure. Senegal, although far from having a genuinely free and responsible press, has built up an atmosphere in which musicians can be critical of affairs at home and abroad. If some, like N'Dour, kept within stylistic boundaries of what he would comment on, others pushed the limits. This edginess has especially been the hallmark of Senegalese rap artists. Using the relatively open political culture to their advantage, groups of this type have called for a greater emphasis on social justice by state officials. In taking on this responsibility the government was put on notice: "We're here with our tongues to correct you when you're not acting right."[26]

This openness reveals that on culture, as in other issue areas, regime type matters. Authoritarian rule, whether of a harsh or benign nature, cuts down on the opportunities for activism outside the purview of the state. Nonstate activity bordering at all on what can be considered diplomatic activity is not accepted. Entertainers are left with choices that range between displaying loyalty or accommodation to the government in power in various ways, maintaining a strict demarcation between the cultural and political spheres, or exiting from the control of the state. A tight distinction is maintained between acceptable cultural activity and politicized activity.

Snapshots from the South reveal how structural impediments from the inside reinforce the external constraints imposed by the Anglo-sphere in muting and distorting the potential of celebrity diplomacy. The choice of loyalty or accommodation permeates the experience of the Middle East. One option is for entertainers to identify themselves completely with a regime, as Umm Kulthum (the mother of modern Arabic music) did with the regime of General Gamal Abdel Nasser in Egypt. A champion of pan-Arabism, Kulthum responded to the trauma of the Six-Day War by becoming a cultural ambassador for the Nasser regime, raising money for the decimated Egyptian armed forces through an extended tour of the Arab world.[27]

Another choice puts entertainers themselves into the position of the disciplinarians of the intersection between the cultural and political dimensions. An interesting case of this phenomenon emerged in the late 1990s with the appointment of Hussein Fahmy, a distinguished Egyptian actor and both a UN messenger of peace and a regional UNDP ambassador, as

the president of the International Film Festival in Cairo. On two fundamental pillars, Fahmy stood firmly behind official policy. On geopolitical
grounds he confirmed the approach with respect to boycotting Israeli films.
Culturally, he drew a firm line against accepting films about homosexuality,
as "they do not suit our moral values and traditions."[28]

The passive option is much harder to identify because of the undetectable
essence of its nonactivity. One illustration in the Middle East entertainment
world that stands out, however, is the case of Haifa Wehbe, the Lebanese
popular singer. Wehbe has not only stayed safely on the sidelines in the
Lebanese conflict, but she has been very careful not even to perform on
sites that would indicate a preference about which side she is on.

Another indication of the severity of these domestic structural impediments comes in the search for members of the Middle Eastern diasporas
to take on the role of UN goodwill ambassadors. Such entertainers are, of
course, attractive in their own right, particularly if they can generate interest
in the UN by younger generations with hybrid identities. But another source
of their appeal is that they can and do speak their minds relatively freely.
The risk remains that these young "ambassadors," if attractive and engaging,
are also naïve and out of their depths in terms of complex issues.

A good example of the positives and negatives of this new approach
surfaces with the appointment of Natacha Atlas—a singer brought up in
Brussels and the UK but who lives in Cairo, sings in Arabic, and had her
major breakthrough in France—as a goodwill ambassador for the UNHCR.
She was young and confident. But her remarks to an interviewer reveal
a mixture of motivations that could cause confusion: "It's not just about
juggling a career and using this as a stepping stone to something else. I'm
not as well known as Geri Halliwell, so I really feel compelled to make a
go of this."[29]

Going on the offensive is also the mark of the approach adopted by regimes that have a preference for state-embedded strategies—but without
authoritarian overtones. The most compelling example is the dominance
of celebrity diplomacy by high-profile members of the Jordanian royal
family. Queen Noor al-Hussein is a prominent participant at Davos, as
well as being active on a number of initiatives relating to war-torn
countries, including the campaign against land mines and refugee issues.
Her focus on reconstruction has included a 2007 visit to Liberia in the
company of George Soros. Queen Raina al-Abdullah is firmly located
in the inner circle of celebrity diplomacy, as exemplified by her appearance in a WEF session "On Hope" with Bono and Emeritus Archbishop
Desmond Tutu. Princess Basma Bint Talal serves as a goodwill ambas-

sador for UNIFEM, UNDP, and UNFPA and is a well-respected and well-networked participant at events such as the UN world conferences on women and population.

Turning the model on its head, however, are representative democratic systems that present internal structural impediments of their own. With the opportunity to participate fully in the political system, some leading celebrities from the South have often been seduced by the temptations of power. Rather than using their reputations to leverage advantage on specific projects—whether working through the UN or as freelance actors—these celebrities have shown an opportunistic streak in wanting to grab the prize of high political office for themselves.

These temptations go well beyond the confines of Africa. One classic instance is the U-turn in the career of Imran Khan. He gained fame both as a cricket star, leading Pakistan to its first and only World Cup title in 1992, and as a man about town in London. But on his return to Pakistan, Imran (as he preferred to be known) changed his image. He divorced his socialite English wife, Jemima Goldsmith (a close friend of Princess Diana), renewed his commitment to Islam, started the sociopolitical Movement for Justice (Tehrik-e-Insaaf in Urdu), and pushed to gain political office.

In looking for the nexus between commitment and opportunism, Imran merits considerable attention. His philanthropic work in trying to set up cancer hospitals and doing reconstruction work for earthquake victims deserves praise. Yet behind all this activity lies an enormous appetite for power. Indeed, when looked at closely, Imran's career appears to be that of a celebrity who had the potential to be a celebrity diplomat but lost appeal over time. Instead of continuing to act as a force of moderation and tolerance, Imran began to pander to a domestic constituency after becoming a candidate in national elections, most notably siding with minority obscurantist voices over unsubstantiated news reports in 2005 regarding U.S. troops flushing the Koran down toilets at Guantanamo. Considerable damage to his global reputation was done after the stories turned out to be incorrect.

Up to that incident, Imran had close links to western NGOs and other financial donor groups who were helping him in his philanthropic work. Through his desire for publicity as a means of winning power, Imran serves as an example of a celebrity from the South brought to ground by the temptations of converting that celebrity status into a position at the apex of power.

Because of the relative openness of some African political systems (compounded by a winner-take-all ethos), the temptations to convert celebrity status into political power is even more pervasive in the region. To be sure, the celebrities discussed in the context of Live 8 resisted this temptation, although the lure was dangled. N'Dour, as might be expected, had both the stature and system structure most readily available for him to take advantage of this conversion process. Many of his concerts ended with the cry, "Youssou pour le président." And he commented forthrightly about this dilemma: "If I can use my position to help my country, then I will. But the music is the thing that sustains me. I can reach more people and at least I don't get up on stage and tell lies."[30]

Although his own uneasiness with the temptation of office is palpable, N'Dour's own sense of serenity could be broken with respect to those entertainers he felt were using their oppositional credentials to position themselves for power. He was particularly scathing about the activities of Fela Anikulapo-Kuti (the late Nigerian musician and social critic), whom he felt was craving the role of an insider while being harsh in his public statements about the political establishment.[31]

N'Dour's refusal to be tempted by the allure of political office must be contrasted finally with the sudden transformation of George Weah. Weah was arguably the best-known African celebrity recruited by the UN to be a goodwill ambassador for UNICEF in 1997. In terms of profile, his credentials were impeccable. While playing football at AC Milan in 1995 he was African, European ("golden ball"), and world player of the year. And with a keen and diverse sense of engagement, he proved a perfect fit for diplomacy. With other famous footballers—Ronaldo and Zidane—he had participated in a massive march against poverty in 2003. He raised money for UNICEF through his participation in the Lively Up Africa recording in 1998. And he was a tremendous philanthropic force in both helping to raise HIV/AIDS awareness and enabling youth to play sports in his home country of Liberia.

Whether due to impatience or overweening ambition, or simply because the opportunity became available, Weah decided to forgo the role of celebrity diplomat to run for the position of president of Liberia. The risks of this choice soon became apparent. Partisanship in a race in which the democratic culture was thin, to say the least, meant having to play the political game without many rules or checks.[32] In any case, Weah ended up a double loser. After pulling ahead in the first round of the presidential elections, he fell short in the runoff vote against Ellen Johnson-Sirleaf (Africa's first elected female leader, who has since become an insider on the Clinton Global Initiative). And the reputation he built up as a dynamic goodwill ambassador was dissipated by what many saw as political opportunism.

PROSPECTS FOR THE DIVERSIFICATION
OF CELEBRITY DIPLOMACY

Amid these twin structural barriers, some evolving forms of authentic agency that may reshape the formation of celebrity diplomacy from the wider ambit of the global South can be detected as well. Some of these innovations link up with changes that are emerging in the North, with regard to with whom and how celebrity diplomats are relocating themselves. A vital element of this process of shape shifting is the introduction of representatives of minorities and diasporas to the enterprise. As will be rehearsed in the conclusion, this dynamic facilitates the release of a new cohort of potential celebrity diplomats, most notably Wyclef Jean and Ronaldinho.

Before moving to explore these possibilities, however, two other trends must be dealt with as alternatives. One is the trend toward a radical form of celebrity diplomacy from the South. Through this lens, celebrity diplomats from the South would reject the notion of reproducing the mode of behavior manufactured and projected by their counterparts in the North. Counterhegemonic voices would come to the fore.

An example of this sort of behavior can be seen in the activities of Arundhati Roy, the Indian author and antiwar critic who served on the World Tribunal on Iraq.[33] In some ways, her confrontational style toward the United States echoes the approach of Harry Belafonte within the United States. A strong public advocate for civil rights as a close collaborator with the Reverend Martin Luther King Jr. and an artist whose own career as a singer and actor did much to cut through the "color barrier" of the entertainment world, Belafonte had acted as a UN goodwill ambassador for UNICEF since 1987 without great incident. Then in January 2006, Belafonte made his role controversial when he went with a number of other activists—including the film star Danny Glover, also a UNICEF goodwill ambassador—as part of a delegation to Venezuela. Appearing with President Hugo Chávez, Belafonte condemned President George W. Bush while praising Chávez's Bolivarian revolution. He added that; "Not hundreds, not thousands, but millions of the American people ... support your revolution."[34]

By taking this step, Belafonte crossed the line of what was judged to be acceptable "diplomatic" behavior. UNICEF quickly released a statement that Belafonte was talking only as a private citizen, not in his capacity as a UN ambassador. He was shunned by other headliners, especially Hillary Clinton, at a joint appearance on behalf of the Children's Defense Fund. As one gossip columnist put it, "Belafonte might have star power, but he doesn't offer the sort of celebrity linkage that helps a politician who's been positioning herself as a right-center Democrat while considering running for President in a couple of years."[35] And he was ridiculed and condemned by the conservative U.S. media as a celebrity whose "public activism has taken him in a new and strident direction as a critic of American foreign policy and a purveyor of a noxious form of anti-Americanism."[36]

At least two components of Roy's ongoing agenda nonetheless differentiate her role from Belafonte's. First, she remains a freelance actor, without either the advantages or disadvantages of UN affiliation. The second is her authentic connection with a specific geographic place. Roy's global role as an antiwar, anti-U.S. activist goes hand in hand with her activism in India on big dams and other issues.

The second trend is a greater orientation toward building connections between celebrities and specific functional activities. The Indian subcontinent provides a valuable laboratory for this type of work. Most notably, a host of Bollywood stars have made themselves available for a combination of confidence-building activities and disaster relief efforts.

As elsewhere, these stars can be separated on the basis of the time span and level of their commitment. Longtime activist Shabana Azmi stands at one end of the spectrum, with a heavy involvement in both local programs (antislum resistance going back to 1980) and global works (removing the stigma of AIDS victims). At the 2006 WEF, the Bollywood star was honored with the prestigious Crystal Award, alongside Michael Douglas. The honor put Shabana Azmi in the same category as Peter Gabriel and Richard Gere, who won the award in previous years.

The move by Amitabh Bachchan (Big B) into this type of public role is of more recent vintage, as he became a goodwill ambassador for UNICEF only in 2005. But given his experience and profile, it was not a huge leap. His main contribution beyond his career as India's best-known man of cinema had been as a multiple brand ambassador. This activity held significant public (lending his name and voice to Indian states) and private dimensions (a large number of commercial endorsements for Indian companies). Not surprisingly, Bachchan proved to be an instant success with a special emphasis on the campaign against polio. His star power was so immense in TV and radio commercials that he was able to convince much of the population to come in for vaccinations. As one woman lining up for her shot relayed what had convinced her to do so: "If I had not come, he [Big B] would have become angry."[37]

Moreover, Bachchan had energy left for some freelance activities as an elder statesman. In terms of confidence building within the subcontinent he advocated fostering better ties between filmmakers of India and Pakistan: "After all, we are the same people, speak the same language, have the same culture."[38] In terms of disaster relief for the 2004 Indian Ocean tsunami, which drew a huge response from Bollywood, Bachchan took part in a six-hour concert in Bombay to raise funds for the victims. The extent of Bachchan's global network power is indicated by his status as an ambassador in Nelson Mandela's 46664 campaign to raise awareness and funds for HIV/AIDS along with Oprah Winfrey, Brad Pitt, and many other celebrities.

TIGHTENING OR LOOSENING THE GRIP OF THE ANGLO-SPHERE

Much of this chapter confirms the tight grip of the model of celebrity diplomacy found in the Anglo-sphere. The measure of this hold acts as a corollary of what is commonly called the soft power held by the dominant states from the North. The attraction of celebrities within the hub is magnified by their vibrant association at the fascinating intersection of popular culture and decision making.

When challenged, however, the hub can retreat behind a more exclusionary regime, a management style that one critic suggests is "a censorship as complete and insidious and ingenious" as ever exerted.[39] If the image of entrapment needs to be taken seriously, so should the breakout strategies exerted in the global South either as a means to coexist with or to counter the Anglo-sphere model. One approach is simply for the South to celebrate its own entertainers as part of an approach that connects Africa as an object of a good deal of celebrity diplomacy to Africans as subjects of interest and inquiry. The impulse to rethink in structural terms the manner in which Africa is presented or not presented to the world is summarized by Ken Wiwa: "The trouble with Live 8 and all this focus on Africa is that it is mostly for western consumption. Live 8 may be global in its ambition, but it is purely for a northern audience. The selection of musicians would not draw a crowd in Ouagadougou or Bambako or Durban and yet we are being sold on an idea that Africa stands at a pivotal moment in our history."[40]

That being said, Africa and the entire global South have already in store a rich array of potential celebrity diplomats who can use their own agency to cut through the structural cracks. Moreover, this production is highly diverse in geographical focus, their niches of operation, and their preferred level of intensity. Although still sui generis, the work of the Mandela Foundation indicates that significant networks can be developed privileging celebrities from the South.

If the supply of celebrity diplomats is accumulating, so is the demand. Paradoxically, the call for celebrity diplomats from the South to take on a bigger role on the global stage may increasingly come from the North. Facing a possible backlash toward their legitimacy, northern-based celebrity diplomats will need to embrace their emerging counterparts from the South. Any notion of celebrity colonialism weighs heavily on an enterprise that holds access and "one-ness" in such high esteem.[41] If celebrity diplomacy is to be accorded accolades over cynicism, ownership must be opened up and distributed beyond a narrow magic circle from the hub Anglo-sphere. Universalism in intent must be matched by universalism in personnel, as any prolonged disconnect between object and subject undermines the fundamental value and sustainability of celebrity diplomacy as a viable project.

Conclusion:
The Contentious Future
of Celebrity Diplomacy

The surge of involvement and interest in celebrity diplomacy has brought with it concern and controversy. Is the work of the celebrity diplomats featured in this book valuable as well as novel? What, if any, added value do these actors bring to the repertoire of diplomacy and global affairs more generally? And how wide and deep does this value extend?

For some sociological theorists, the logic of celebrities entering the domain of diplomacy is unassailable. Under the accelerating forces of globalization, the distance between citizens and sites of power has widened. Celebrities provide a convenient surrogate for, and a conduit in response to, the traditional bonds that hold society together, performing mobilizing, interpreting, and, most importantly, mediating functions that have been eroded within traditional institutions.[1] Nowhere is this need for new forms of mediation more apparent than in the world of diplomacy. Quite self-consciously, official diplomatic culture has been developed without the formation of solid links to domestic society. The language of "estrangement," or in a more convoluted fashion, "disintermediation," has been increasingly invoked to describe this state of disconnect.[2]

In the domain of public diplomacy and/or advocacy, those officials who are bounded by national structures are at a huge competitive disadvantage, compared to celebrities who have become engaged on issues related to global public policy. Official diplomats seek to engage publics in an increasingly comprehensive fashion, with a playbook that gives greater emphasis to moving beyond intergovernmental processes. But the basic instinct of these same diplomats is to marshal and husband information, not to share it. Even if they wanted to, they could not attract or talk to massive audiences. Their comfort level is with selective/targeted domains, not the type of publics found in hyper-events such as the Live 8 concerts, or through MTV, the *Oprah Winfrey Show,* and other such open-ended vehicles of communication.

Celebrities are more akin to some components of the NGO sphere in what has been termed the struggle to "occupy the mind space" of people around the world.[3] However, on the basis of this comparison, celebrities possess some clear presentational advantages. Some NGOs such as Oxfam have extensive brand recognition and fund-raising abilities. But in mobilization terms they remain faceless organizations. On the basis of the power of attraction, therefore, NGOs are subordinated to celebrities. As observers on the ground continually acknowledge in the abstract, "When a celebrity talks, people listen; there is no better messenger."[4] Or, for that matter, from an explicitly comparative organizational perspective: "They can reach into people's lives and speak to them in ways that Oxfam spokesmen cannot. They can reach out to people who might not normally listen to what Oxfam has to say."[5]

Detractors (particularly among the champions of the orthodox diplomatic culture) acknowledge the proliferation of a new form of outsiders into this realm but see this movement not as the "next big thing" but as a distraction. Something may be happening, whereby: "First-class airport lounges are now crowded with rock-star diplomats, spokesmodels and 'actors without borders.'"[6] But it should be treated as a fad that will ultimately fade away under the weight of its conceptual contradictions and operational fragility.

Instead of buying into the logic of celebrities playing a useful and inevitable task in a diffuse world, the elevation of celebrities into the domain of global affairs is treated as another symptom of "our galloping fetishisation" of this cohort.[7] The dumbing down of other modes of public life is bad enough, but the intrusion of enthusiastic amateurs into the turf of professional diplomats is populism run amok. "Celebocracy" can grab and hold the attention of mass publics. But the result is simply an exercise in superficial froth at best and policy distortion at worst.

By its very nature, this type of debate is irreconcilable. The pros and cons exist in two solitudes with little or no room for merger. For the promoters of celebrities, this phenomenon represents an inexorable force tied in with the onward rush of globalization, with all its attendant elements of mass technology in global communications. Structure is everything. For the resisters the challenge is cast as part of an opportunistic spillover from the wider celebrity culture, with the global stage providing an inviting place for public stunts and self-indulgence. The issue is not about systemic change in the profile of diplomacy, it is about a flawed form of agency.

To tease out the authentic importance of celebrity diplomacy, with respect to both its positive and negative connotations, means extending the level of analysis beyond these parameters. Attempts to trivialize celebrity diplomacy may paradoxically feed an image that discounts a bigger set of difficulties with the enterprise. If it is not accorded the serious treatment it deserves, governance issues that exist beyond the prerogatives of official diplomacy will remain out of bounds for scrutiny. The retention of this "no go" arena does nobody any good, including the celebrity diplomats who are involved in a steep learning curve.

Nor, it should be added, is it fair to offer a caricature of celebrity diplomacy in which a roster of stars are lumped in together with little or no care to differentiate between vastly different types of attributes and projects. Diplomacy is a complex activity with a vast array of actors. So too is the celebrity diplomacy that I have explored in this book.

ONE SIZE DOES NOT FIT ALL: THE GLAMOROUS ENTHUSIASTS

One of the major objectives of this project is to explore the sheer variety among those individuals who can be termed celebrity diplomats. The presence of so many actors who signal some intention of being celebrity diplomats both extends, and in some cases debases, the currency of celebrity diplomacy. By this measure any celebrity that makes any pronouncement about any global issue attracts attention, however silly or incomplete.

Furthermore, the problem of celebrity diplomats as "loose cannons" must be addressed. As noted, some figures in this category have been enormously successful in framing issues. One only needs to be reminded again of Princess Diana on the issue of land mines and Richard Gere on Tibet. The difficulty comes when the loose cannon has some associative status with the UN as a goodwill ambassador. Gerri Halliwell stands out as testimony that these programs are only as good as the weakest link. Furthermore, the possibility of surprises always lurks around the corner, as the controversy over Harry Belafonte suggests. A long-standing and apparently benign presence is turned overnight into an avalanche of negative publicity.

Although this is not an academic book with a strict methodology, some definitional clarity about who should be included in the category of celebrity diplomats is required. Madonna, Kate Moss, and even Paris Hilton were present either as performers or observers of Live 8, but presence alone does not make them celebrity diplomats. As noted in Chapter 1, recognition is in part a self-appointed status. It needs to be embellished, though, with activity that rubs up against the official world of diplomacy. Talking is not enough, even though the communicative function can be crucial. Simply endorsing or giving to a charity—in whatever generous a fashion in terms of time or money—also falls short of the mark. The value of many of these philanthropic activities must be acknowledged, but contributions of this type by themselves are not what celebrity diplomacy is about. And some of this work may go terribly wrong. As witnessed by the wave of distaste over Madonna's crude ventures into Africa, through the building of orphanages and the adoption of "Baby David" in Malawi, the possibility of a contamination of the brand is a distinct possibility.

The power of agency—and both its adaptive capabilities and contentious possibilities—is captured by the continued rise of Angelina Jolie. At the outset of her involvement with the UNHCR, it might have been expected that Jolie would have been a magnified version of Ginger Spice. With all her self-doubt and arguably self-destructiveness, combined with the bubble life of a Hollywood star, a good bet might have been placed on her to do exactly what the critics predicted: flame out as a putative diplomat. The possibility seemed far higher for embarrassment than kudos. As Jolie recounted, the initial response among UN field workers was one of profound skepticism: "They don't dumb it down for an actress. They said ... we did have bets as to how much luggage you'd have and would you be wearing high heels ... and we did sit around and wonder, what was this kind of strange creature that was coming to the middle of a place that seemed not to fit at all."[8]

Instead of revealing the weaknesses of the enterprise, Angelina Jolie has exhibited many of the potential strengths, in part because of her ability to mix art and real life. Starring in adventure films in exotic locations provided added credibility to her front-line activity both as a UN goodwill ambassador and her more recent ventures into freelance diplomatic activity. It also reflected an immense amount of personal growth and maturity caused by motherhood and a growing appreciation of what her role could be. As Jolie readily acknowledged: "[I've] changed a lot in the last few years. I've traveled a lot, I've learned a lot, my view of the world is different."[9]

Agency does not mean untrammeled individual autonomy. Part of the Angelina Jolie narrative is about personal growth. But behind her—and a good deal of the other celebrity diplomats—is a substantive amount of organizational backing. When she appeared for a special two-hour edition of *Anderson Cooper 360°*, Jolie's remarks were well rehearsed.[10] Angelina Jolie's advisor on international affairs is Trevor Neilson, who served on

DATA's founding board of directors and as the director of public affairs for the Gates Foundation. Any sense, therefore, that Jolie is some kind of naïve actor working from an off-the-cuff script is very misleading. In a sharp rebuttal to any image of frivolity, Jolie told the Davos audience: "You shouldn't assume you should be taken seriously just because your heart's in the right place. Celebrities have a responsibility to know what they are talking about and be in it for the long run."[11]

Amid these strengths, however, the risks remain hyper-charged. Angelina Jolie's public profile as a good international citizen is always in danger of being overwhelmed by the volatility or foibles of her personal life, especially when these different roles get jumbled together. Jolie herself could become overstretched by trying to keep these different roles on track, necessitating a cutback in her engagements. Alternatively, the welcome mat for her could be removed by countries in the South due either to a generalized backlash toward her as simply another face of western domination or because of negative reactions to specific incidents surrounding her visits. Jolie's decision to have her child with Brad Pitt in Namibia may have helped the tourist industry, but it made her a target of critical fire. According to one commentator, Jolie's trip was a "grotesque manifestation of colonial privilege.... [She] essentially dictated security measures to a sovereign country, taking advantage of its poverty in order to have a "special" experience giving birth in Africa. She decided who entered and left the country and carved out an exclusive space where she commanded a small army of private security officers."[12]

The other risk flows from her evolving relationship with the established diplomatic culture. With Jolie's ascendancy as a glamorous enthusiast, some competitive pressures were placed on her in terms of her connection with the UNHCR. As with Princess Diana, one option before Jolie is to extend her scope of activity via engagement with NGOs on contentious issues such as Darfur (with her call not only for assistance but also justice through indictments of war criminals). The other scenario, though, is one of embrace or even entrapment by national diplomatic systems along the lines of Bob Geldof. Jolie has increasingly shown a willingness to share the stage with ambitious statesmen, such as Gordon Brown from the UK. She has also been nominated for a five-year term at the Council on Foreign Relations, as part of a program to "nurture the next generation of foreign policy makers."[13] Although such patterns of socialization allow Jolie to gain a more sophisticated appreciation of diplomacy, they also open up the possibility of suffocation wherein her voice might be overwhelmed by the volume of elite expression.

The cluster of celebrity diplomats, then, is never a set affair. Attention needs to be devoted to why and how actors drop off the radar, due either to fatigue or an awkward fit. Equally, though, the maturation process needs to be traced by examining the contours of participation by emergent actors. An interesting illustration of the continuous ramping up of the project is the appearance of George Clooney as a galvanizing figure on the Darfur issue. Clooney studied the art of diplomacy as practiced by Bono and Jolie for a good length of time before jumping into the game himself (limiting himself to a small speech at the Murrayfield Live 8 concert). But once he jumped, he did so with full force. He picked an issue that was ripe for a major initiative. And one that in U.S. terms had a good deal of potential for bipartisan backing, with calls for humanitarian intervention coming from liberals and the Christian right. It was an issue as well that called out for support from the African American community, as evoked by Clooney's much publicized appearance on the *Oprah Winfrey Show*.

Clooney's foray into celebrity diplomacy not only belies its faddish image in terms of the amount of rehearsal time, replete with his trip (accompanied by his father, Nick Clooney, a former television journalist) to the Darfur region. It also cuts into, if not completely eliminates, the superficial critique. Foreign policy commentators might disagree with his analysis, and many did. Still, they had to treat him as a serious actor even when they attacked his operational template. A flavor of these critiques is garnered from one rebuttal: "Rarely does [Clooney] criticize any other governments by name—not even the government of Sudan, the author of the genocide. His discussion of the facts of Darfur focuses on the victims and on the United States, not on the perpetrators in Sudan and their abettors in China, the Arab League, and the UN."[14]

Other celebrities addressed these criticisms in a more direct fashion. Clooney's *Ocean's* franchise costar Don Cheadle has made action on the Darfur crisis a personal priority. An acclaimed actor in his own right, Cheadle's credibility on human rights is largely associated with his lead role in *Hotel Rwanda*, and he has directed his influence toward a sophisticated awareness campaign. Teaming up with John Prendergast, senior advisor to the International Crisis Group and a former advisor to the Clinton administration, he wrote the best-selling book *Not on Our Watch*, about the Darfur genocide. Charting simple strategies to empower everyday citizens with the tools to force change, Cheadle and Prendergast have reached out to an energetic and internationally conscious audience eager to compel action. Unlike Clooney's efforts, the focus of this mobilization (as part of the Save Darfur Coalition) was placed squarely on punitive measures "with teeth" against the Khartoum regime.[15]

In a similar spirit, Mia Farrow, the star of *Rosemary's Baby*, has added creative diplomatic leverage to this campaign, targeting not only the government of Sudan but its major ally and protectorate at the UN Security Council, China.[16] In March 2007, Farrow penned an op-ed in the *Wall Street Journal* in which she indicted China's efforts to block action in Darfur and called out Hollywood director Steven Spielberg for his involvement in the 2008 Beijing Olympics, igniting a firestorm of commentary in traditional media outlets and on the Internet through blogs and YouTube. Farrow's strategy was a calculated one, having compelled Spielberg to raise the issue with Chinese President Hu Jintao, who then in turn persuaded Khartoum to accept a UN peacekeeping force. She used the network with which she is familiar to gain access to a network of influence. Analogous to the approach forged by Bono, Farrow is representative of a growing cast of celebrities that has challenged the traditional assumptions of quiet diplomacy.[17]

BONO AND BOUNDARY-SPANNING NETWORKS

Where the critics of celebrity diplomacy miscalculate in their analysis is in conflating Bono and his wider network with the host of glamorous enthusiasts. Bono may be judged to have his faults. They are not the faults, nonetheless, commonly ascribed to the generic class of Hollywood celebrity diplomats. As Henry Kissinger is to official diplomacy, Bono is to celebrity diplomacy. Kissinger raised the bar of state-centric diplomacy with the prioritization of high politics and the identification of the national interest. In organizational terms, his greatest concern was with his own exclusive managerial functions. Bono relishes complexity and contradictions in his public and private lives. Access is placed far above control. Instead of management, the onus is put on entrepreneurship on an issue-specific basis. The power of voice rather than coercion is the tool of choice. And at odds with the salience given to status and hierarchy, evolving types of relationships are utilized. Kissinger can be cast as the diplomat cum celebrity who vigorously performed as the classic gatekeeper. Bono is the emergent celebrity diplomat who acts as a new type of boundary-spanner.[18]

The idea expressed by some critics that Bono should go back to his "day job"—what Eric Clapton would contend is his real profession, that of a member of U2, not the Davos supergroup—has no accurate bearing on the hybridization of his activities. Albeit not without some tensions with his bandmates, his day job increasingly revolves around the functions attendant to his role as a significant actor in international public policy.

His two lives are connected by his charisma and his ingrained sense of spirituality. They run in parallel with the need for very different skill sets. Indeed, Bono went to great pains not to mix the two worlds up. Any whiff of the enthusiastic amateur has been eradicated in his drive for professionalism. Unlike Angelina Jolie, Bono is not a generous donor of his own money to his causes. Bono mobilizes and channels the resources of his more wealthy backers—including, of course, those two other high-profile celebrity diplomats, Bill Gates and George Soros—through activities organized by DATA.

What any profile of Bono reveals is how extensively networked he has become in his activities. Viewed from around the outer edges, the ambit of his operations looks like a mix of loose couplings. Bono has moved from a celebrity who needed mentoring to a celebrity who does the mentoring. When George Clooney or Brad Pitt or other celebrities such as Matt Damon search for guidance on how to become a celebrity diplomat, they go to Bono and DATA. Moreover, this network has been expanded to take on the outlines of a global dimension. Youssou N'Dour is the best-known African celebrity who belongs in this network.

At the core of this activity is not an institutionalized form of club, like the associative efforts of the glamorous enthusiasts around the pillars of the UN. Rather it is a network, with DATA as its hub. Instead of a tight structure—with something still of a guild attached to it, as would be expected within the confines of official diplomacy—this system works in a loose fashion with little day-to-day coordination but a full appreciation of what a combination of resources (both material and knowledge-based) can achieve in terms of symbolic and instrumental delivery.

THE SWEEP OF QUESTIONS BEYOND SUPERFICIALITY

Viewed in this more expansive fashion, it is not the superficiality of celebrity diplomacy that needs closer examination but the superficiality of the dismissal by its critics. The sweep of questions associated with celebrity diplomacy may actually be more expansive than what the most visible critics have asked. Viewing it through the diplomatic lens, they make charges of faddism, but celebrity diplomacy can be opened up to other, more serious deficiencies when scrutinized through the lens of governance.

One obvious point of contention is the level of autonomy these actors have and whether celebrity diplomats (most notably Bono and Bob Geldof) have been co-opted by the state authorities. It reverts to Bianca Jagger's notion of "sleeping with the enemy." In this alternative perspective, the dots are connected in a very different fashion than in the image of a networked boundary spanner. Instead of privileging the dynamics of Bono's own hub via DATA and other activities, the exclusive focus is on what is taken to be the cozying-up behavior toward Bush, Blair, and the G8 summit.

Such a view, if accurate at all, mixes up the boundary-spanning network of Bono and the more idiosyncratic activities of Geldof. To his credit, Geldof brought to the enterprise a good many positive attributes, above all his marvelous (if often over the top) sense of public relations. His vulnerability was his love of attention by the high and mighty. His report card on the G8 reflected this craving. So did his subsequent shift from the Blair/Brown axis to become an advisor for David Cameron, the Conservative's up-and-coming leader, on his Global Poverty Group.[19]

Geldof has been at his best when he played the "bad cop" to Bono's "good cop." When he revived this abrasive role, notably at the 2007 G8, the strengths of his personality (as opposed to the flaws) came to the fore. One of these strengths was his ability to speak the language of the street, transpositioning the sentiment of those on the other side of the summit's fences to an elevated forum. As Bono went upmarket, editing special editions of the *Independent,* the French newspaper *Libération,* and *Vanity Fair,* Geldof reproduced this activity through the tabloids. Most dramatically, he edited the best-selling German tabloid *Bild Zeitung* on the eve of the summit, redirecting the attention of its audience away from its usual fare of sports scores and scantily clad models to the crisis in Africa. At the celebrity press conference at the end of the Heiligendamm summit, Geldof left detailed criticism of the communiqué to Bono. Instead he injected an emotional sense of disappointment about the failure of the G8 leaders to live up to their Gleneagles promises. Bono commented on the technical deficiencies of the summit outcomes document, dismissing it as having been "deliberately designed not to communicate." Geldof loudly and sweepingly condemned the proceedings as a "total farce."[20] By his willingness to speak out so passionately about the failure of delivery from Gleneagles to Heiligendamm, Geldof won back the grudging respect of some of his critics who had dismissed him as a co-opted figure who sought too close connections with Tony Blair and the political establishment more generally. Although the coordinator of the European antiglobalization network Attac was not willing to forget Geldof's "premature" signal at Gleneagles that the battle against poverty had been won, he also suggested that Geldof's more critical approach at Heiligendamm helped extend the antipoverty message.[21]

This rehabilitation was accentuated by Geldof's willingness at the Heiligendamm summit to give equal standing to representatives from the global South. Youssou N'Dour was given a prominent place in the lobbying efforts directed at the G8 leaders with Geldof and Bono. In an attempt to cleanse the memory of the closed, Anglo-centric environment of the Live 8 concert, musicians from the global South were given ample time on stage at the huge Raise Your Voice against Poverty concert in Rostock (dubbed the P8, or Poverty 8), held the first night of the leaders' summit.

Bono's approach, however, remains more sophisticated, flexible, and sustainable. His mantra is to continually play key political leaders off each other, balancing intense involvement with an eye to keeping the boundaries of access open to as many decision makers as possible. Nudging and cajoling go hand in hand with maintaining a presence in core policy circles. Public rebukes are reserved for the smaller players or those that were on their way out of power. The G8 summit provides a state-centric target. Davos provides the core site for deepening the "logic of the network society" as conceptualized by Manuel Castells.[22]

The potential problem with the Bono network is not its intrusion into public space. The bilateral relationship Bono forged with Bush and Blair—and his privileged access with Geldof at the Gleneagles summit both physically (via helicopter) and symbolically (in terms of their presence at the communiqué signing)—may indicate a formal appreciation of the mobilizing, channeling, and mediating role of celebrity diplomacy. But it did not create a crisis in governance, in that Bono's meetings were media-driven and hoisted on the back of the unique Live 8 "mandate" that a message on debt and development assistance be delivered to the G8 leaders.

The greater potential difficulty with the network, encompassing not only Bono but also the Gates Foundation (infused with the astronomical gift of $31 billion plus from Warren Buffett)[23] and the Open Society Institute, is not the dynamics of its relationship with state officials at the apex of power but the nature of its own inner workings as an expression of the ascendancy of private authority on global public policy.[24] The unbundling of the state and the assumption by celebrities of the role of a filter or conduit between citizens and sites of authority is one thing. The question of accountability and the representative form of this network (with its privileged access not just to policy makers but to the mass media, and its combination of popular legitimacy and massive material resources) is another thing entirely.

The question of asymmetrical representation has already been touched on in connection with the divide between the insider celebrity diplomats and those excluded from the magic circle. As noted by reference to the Anglo-sphere, that issue mirrors the North-South divide. But it also reflects a differentiated pattern across racial lines within the Anglo-sphere itself.

As on the North-South divide, the bias goes beyond the issue of structural constraints. A number of prominent African Americans have as much potential to be celebrity diplomats as the cohort depicted in the core of this book. Some stars from this background avoid extending their role by their own volition, however, mindful that such associations could put restrictions on their autonomous activities. Danny Glover, the well-known African American Hollywood star, is perhaps the prototype of this type of thinking. When asked "Is Glover the New Bono?" by a South African journalist, the star of *Lethal Weapon* and other box office hits demurred, saying that his preferred role was to act as "an obnoxious radical" and spokesperson for the dispossessed. In tune with this alternative role, Glover traveled with Harry Belafonte to Caracas to attend the WSF where they met Chávez.[25]

One potential lever by which diversity can be opened up in the ranks of celebrity diplomats is the world of sports. A stand-out candidate from this sector is Ronaldinho, the transplanted Brazilian football/soccer star. He has not only enormous appeal as a sportsman (including the award World/European Player of the Year) but enormous credibility as someone who has risen from poverty in the favelas (Brazilian slums) while remaining connected to his roots. His role as a World Food Program ambassador in Latin America reveals his interest in taking on significant public roles. But equally significant is the support he has from his athletic club, as Futbol Club Barcelona has become the first team to have UN sponsorship, complete with the UNICEF logo on the front of their jersey. Under the deal—eagerly endorsed by Ronaldinho—Barcelona agreed to contribute $1.9 million to UNICEF humanitarian projects, bearing the slogan on their jerseys: "Barcelona, more than a club, a new global hope for vulnerable children."[26]

A second, enormously attractive strand is the robustness of hip-hop. The music mogul Russell Simmons stands out as a pivotal figure who could act as a conduit into this culture. Simmons played a large role in putting the Philadelphia Live 8 concert together. He also became involved in the enormous Washington, D.C., rally on the Darfur crisis that featured George Clooney and a wide number of other notables across the spectrum of political and entertainment worlds.

In terms of context, Simmons acknowledged that hip-hop could be a potent tool of mobilization in global affairs. As he commented, individual stars from this component of the musical world are "more important than Kofi Annan right now to a lot of young people. So these celebrities need to be put in the middle of these kinds of missions."[27]

The major hip-hop star who did become a core member of the Bono network was not Simmons but a star rapper with a very different profile: Wyclef Jean. The distinctive quality about Wyclef was his membership in the Haitian diaspora. The name of the group that made him famous was the Fugees, short for refugees. His concerns have blended the generalized outlook of many other celebrity diplomats (compassion and a sense of justice on global poverty) with a specific niche vis-à-vis the reconstruction of his home island. Brought up as a member of a double minority in Brooklyn, Wyclef has done more than any other celebrity in drawing attention to the plight of Haiti through the work of his Yéle Haiti foundation.

Wyclef's sense of commitment drew a wide number of celebrities into his orbit. Most famously, he attracted Angelina Jolie and Brad Pitt to visit Haiti in January 2006 as a sign of support for his work on the ground. Much of his inspiration, however, came from Bono, whom he credits as being his mentor.[28]

Wyclef has demonstrated the potential of utilizing these connections. He collaborated with Bono on an upbeat single, "New Day," created for NetAid, an online partnership between Cisco Systems and the UNDP. Operationally, he followed Bono's lead by moving substantially past the standard model of other hip-hop artists who do one-time events as gestures of concern. What he wanted to do was what Bono had achieved: galvanize.[29]

Unfortunately in terms of context, Wyclef dug into the same trough of cynicism about the motivations of celebrities that straddle the line between entertainment and public involvement. Some commentators tried to tarnish Wyclef's reputation with references to the links that other members of his family had to malevolent political forces in Haiti.[30] Others wondered if he was simply using his foundation as a platform for his own political ambitions in a manner reminiscent of Imran Khan and George Weah.[31] Fairly or unfairly, such attitudes point to the self-imposed restrictions on the maturing of celebrity diplomacy.

Controversy over the question of accountability has been accentuated by Bono's championing of the Product Red brand since January 2006. Announced, as with so many other initiatives at the major site of celebrity diplomacy, Davos, it is a campaign designed to involve specific components of the private sector (including Armani, Gap, Motorola, and Converse/Nike) in order to increase funds and awareness for the Global Fund in order to fight AIDS and other diseases in Africa. Although it is still a relatively new project, the core notion behind it is that this portfolio of companies would donate a percentage of sales from select products bearing the Red mark to the Global Fund, the public-private partnership whose biggest supporter is the Gates Foundation.

Bono and DATA sold the Product Red concept as an idea whose time had come. As noted in Chapter 5, Bono explicitly distanced himself from the older generation of activists. In the same vein, Bono wedded the larger struggle against poverty to an upgraded variant of corporate social responsibility: "Red can't make a crap company into a bright light. But if you take two equal firms, Red can help one shine brighter."[32]

Scattered signs of uneasiness with Bono's "insistence on joining hands with global moguls" had been evident from the time he took center stage at the WEF meeting in New York at the beginning of 2002.[33] The Product Red campaign brought out a more systemic display of concern, if not outright resistance.

For some critics, the main objection was the well-rehearsed line that Bono was taking states and their leaders off the hook by putting the emphasis on the blend of big business and conscientious consumers to rescue the impoverished. It was an especially sensitive issue because a mainstay of the initiative, Nike, had come under intense scrutiny for its labor practices.

For others, the problem lay in tracking the more nuanced contradictions between the purported beneficial aim of this initiative and its lack of transparency and accountability. What might in principle be a good idea still raised a number of points of interrogation about its operational practices. Backers of the Product Red campaign were initially reluctant to make public the proportion of profits from Red products that are to be sent to the Global Fund, claiming that it was dependent on sales and the success of the overall campaign. For a campaign built around such high-end commercial products as Apple's iPod and Emporio Armani sunglasses and watches, the returns (even as a percentage of profit on these goods) are sparing. Each iPod Nano Red sold brings in only $10 (or 2 percent of the MP3 player's retail price) to the Global Fund. American Express's Red credit card donates 1 percent of accumulated charges, and the company declines to reveal whether any of the interest on outstanding balances will be donated.[34]

As presented, therefore, the initiative risks contaminating Bono not just superficially ("saving" Africa and Africans by buying a Red T-shirt from Gap made in Botswana, for example) but in a deeper morass of concerns about who really benefits from the campaign. As one NGO representative was quoted in the *Independent*: "You have to admire Bono's creativity but there is a risk that this will ultimately alienate consumers and supporters.

Unless it is very clear that a generous portion of what they spend on the T-shirt or pair of shades is going to fight AIDS or malaria, then they are going to feel they are pouring money into the coffers of corporations who are getting the kudos of fighting poverty at a bargain price."[35]

These specific objections were joined by both a very personalized and a far more generalized attack on Bono and the Product Red initiative. The first line of criticism emphasized the contradictions between the glow of Bono's public idealism and his hard-edged private commercial practices. Detailed investigations have probed Bono's own business empire, the operating principles of which are to minimize taxes as well as diversify investment via real estate, a network of companies and trusts, a private equity firm (Elevation Partners LP), and stakes in Nude (a chain of Dublin cafés) and Edun, the fashion label created with his wife.[36] His calculating approach to building and maintaining this empire and to maximizing his assets is not something that he plays up to his mass audience. The second takes issue at Bono's Product Red campaign for submerging and distorting the issues of AIDS and poverty in and through consumerism. According to the analytical framework of one study, "Product RED's consumers can position themselves as holding a status above everybody with designer products that do not represent the exploitation of the most downtrodden—these products actually help them. Brand Aid creates a world where it is possible to have as much as you want without depriving anybody else."[37]

Rather than reacting defensively to these criticisms, Bono has moved to ramp the campaign up to another level. Enlisting the help of the leading arbiter of popular taste in the United States, Oprah Winfrey—and an additional bevy of celebrities ranging from Penelope Cruz to Kanye West—Bono took Product Red to middle America. Walking down the Magnificent Mile of Michigan Avenue of Chicago, Bono and his entourage went on a massive shopping binge of Product Red brand products. Amid such orchestration—complete with a duet of "Don't Give Up (Africa)" by Bono and Alicia Keys—the marriage of personal indulgence and collective good seemed solid, notwithstanding all the perceived flaws deemed to be embedded in this sort of activity.[38]

CELEBRATING CELEBRITY DIPLOMACY

Whereas critics condemn the phenomenon mainly on the charge of superficiality, celebrity diplomacy is rationalized and lauded by it promoters for its symbolic and instrumental use as a tool of mediation. Celebrity endorsement cuts through the complexity and conventional practices of global affairs. Whether flawed or not, the Product Red campaign illustrates how a new issue or practice is suddenly grabbed by celebrities. The catalytic role of celebrities embellishes the image of mediation, with this type of big and entertaining personality acting as a go-between for society at the mass level and institutional mechanisms that remain biased toward the elite. As one perceptive newspaper editorial phrased it, in the context of George Clooney's intervention on Darfur:

> By its very nature, celebrity diplomacy invites skepticism. How do the rich and famous get off thinking they can flit in and accomplish in a few days what the professional diplomats, government officials and relief workers have struggled with for years? But there's one thing celebrities can do that the diplomats and relief workers can't. They can focus the entire world's attention on a problem, and they can help build a groundswell of public support for the work that the professionals are doing.[39]

If a useful device, though, the image of mediation does not offer a complete picture of the benefits that celebrities can provide. The exposure of some deficiencies within the enterprise does not signify that its embedded strengths should not be celebrated as well. These capabilities go well beyond the role of conduit, to different positive attributes both of process and psychology.

Celebrities provide a different script about how diplomacy is practiced that cannot at all be dismissed as woolly-headed or utopian. On the contrary, the best celebrity diplomats have figured out far more successfully than their professional counterparts how a sophisticated form of public diplomacy can be operated. Direct appeals to a massive public audience are at the core of this approach. If, as John Ruggie notes, a new form of competition has taken shape in the global public domain in which state and nonstate actors vie with each other for attention and imagination, celebrities are well situated in this struggle.[40] For their repertoire consists of an attractive blend of direct and dynamic expression well anchored in norms and expectations. But in parallel with this focus on discourse goes a concerted effort to open doors to as many elite policy makers as possible. This script follows a model proposed by some leading architects of innovative governance, in which the essence of public diplomacy is taken to be "lobbying and policy exchange organizations which link up ... across borders ... creat[ing] public space ... engaging with the domestic politics of other countries [and] with NGOs to change public opinion."[41]

Innovative practices struggle with faddishness in terms of the impact of celebrities on the script of global affairs. Celebrities not only blur but effectively break down the barriers between domestic and international politics. The limits of holding to a firm inside/outside way of thinking and acting are exposed by actors who can readily access so many vehicles of global communication and mechanisms of power. The hallmark of the networks and circuits created and channeled by celebrity diplomats is the freshness and fluidity of their operations. The buzz of the power of discourse, with an eye especially to persuade and shape debate, intersects with the bite of the mobilization of vast material resources. The octane provided by celebrity diplomats meshes increasingly well with a substantive content.

In terms of their psychological outlook, celebrities aim high. By orientation, diplomacy continues to be the art of the possible. Notwithstanding all of their flaws, whether due to oversized egos seeking applause or deficiencies of governance structures in their style of networking, celebrities do raise the level of expectations. Celebrities central to this book want to do more, tilting from the boundaries of the possible to catalytic visions of what is necessary. They may in many cases be tilting against the proverbial windmills with respect to the ever-present myopia of ideas, interests, and institutions in world politics. Yet their presence as participants who look, behave, and speak very differently than those actors who traditionally occupy the elevated space on global affairs says much about how these orthodox assumptions are no longer valid.

Notes

CHAPTER 1

1. *PBS Homepage,* "Benjamin Franklin—World of Influence, Celebrity," 2002, http://www.pbs.org/benfranklin/l3_world_celebrity.html (accessed April 11, 2007).

2. For some recent views on the representative function of official diplomats, see Christer Jönsson and Martin Hall, *Essence of Diplomacy: Studies in Diplomacy and International Relations* (New York: Palgrave, 2005); G. R. Berridge, *Diplomacy: Theory and Practice,* 3rd ed. (New York: Palgrave, Basingstoke, 2005).

3. The case that "we are all diplomats" is given some credence in Richard Langhorne, "Current Developments in Diplomacy: Who Are the Diplomats Now?" *Diplomacy and Statecraft* 8, no. 2 (July 1997), 1–15.

4. On the theme of estrangement in post-Westphalian diplomacy, see James Der Derian, *On Diplomacy: A Genealogy of Western Estrangement* (Oxford: Basil Blackwell, 1987).

5. Angela Ndalianis and Charlotte Henry, eds., *Stars in Our Eyes: The Star Phenomenon in the Contemporary Era* (Westport, CT: Praeger, 2002), vii.

6. On the U.S. phenomenon, see Darrell M. West and John Orman, *Celebrity Politics* (New York: Prentice Hall, 2002).

7. For their own retrospective perspectives on the use of statecraft, see Henry Kissinger, *Diplomacy* (New York: Simon and Schuster, 1994); and Richard C. Holbrooke, *To End a War* (New York: Random House, 1998).

8. Joshua Chaffin, "The Prime-Time Philanthropist," *Financial Times,* January 6–7, 2007. See also Sherryl Wilson, *Oprah, Celebrity, and Formations of Self* (New York: Palgrave, 2003). In addition to Clooney, acclaimed actors Don Cheadle and Mia Farrow have both lobbied for international action in Darfur. Although done in different ways, both Cheadle and Farrow have used the media to raise awareness, calling for citizen-led action.

9. DiCaprio's movie, *Blood Diamond,* has released a wide range of emotions. NGOs such as Global Witness that are pushing for an extension of the Kimberley Process (the mechanism by which gems are provided with a certificate stating where they came from) have used the film to raise awareness about the ongoing seriousness of the issue. Other groups and individuals—whether the World Diamond Council or Nelson Mandela, have preferred to cast the diamond industry as vital to African development. Jeevan Vasagar, "Hollywood Caught in Gem Warfare," *Guardian Weekly,* September 29, 2006.

10. Head of policy at Oxfam, quoted in Charlotte Denny, "Do Celebrities Hurt the Cause?" *Manchester Guardian Weekly,* March 20, 2002.

11. Oxfam International, "Celebrities at World Social Forum Publicly Support Global Call to Action against Poverty," *Oxfam Press Release,* January 29, 2005.

12. For one academic critique, see Jörg Friedrichs, "Global Governance as the Hegemonic Project of Transatlantic Civil Society," in Markus Lederer and Philipp S. Müller, eds., *Criticizing Global Governance* (New York: Palgrave, 2005), 45–68.

13. Melik Kaylan, "In the Fray: Demonstrating Irrelevance: Celebrity Activists," *Wall Street Journal,* February 19, 2003, D16.

14. In this made-for-TV movie, a member of the official UK delegation to the 2005 G8 summit meets a young woman at a café and is convinced by her that the issue of world poverty must be seriously addressed. A German version, *Fruehstueck mit einer Unbekannten,* was made to coincide with the 2007 Heiligendamm summit.

15. Even with this staying power in Europe, questions have been asked about the ongoing status of public intellectuals, especially in the Anglo-sphere. One of the casualties of the ascendancy of celebrity diplomacy may be traditional forms of public intellectuals. See Richard A. Posner, *Public Intellectuals: A Study of Decline* (Cambridge, MA: Harvard University Press, 2001); and Amitai Etzioni and Alyssa Bowditch, *Public Intellectuals: An Endangered Species?* (Lanham, MD: Rowman and Littlefield, 2006).

16. Geldof quoted in Paul Vallely, "All He Wants Now Is a Life to Call His Own," *Independent (London),* July 15, 1995. Jan Aart Scholte notes in his comprehensive examination of globalization that the geography of the entertainment industry, akin to those of financial crises, environmental problems, and human rights, unfolds significantly on a global world scale. *Globalization: A Critical Introduction* (New York: Palgrave, 2005), 59–75.

17. For one sophisticated analysis, see Strobe Talbott, "Globalization and Diplomacy: A Practitioner's Perspective," *Foreign Policy* 108 (Fall 1997), 68–83.

18. See Langhorne, "Current Developments in Diplomacy."

19. James Eayrs, "The Deliquescence of Diplomacy," in *Diplomacy and Its Discontents* (Toronto: University of Toronto Press, 1971), 77.

20. Ibid.

21. Paul Theroux, "The Rock Star's Burden," *New York Times,* December 19, 2005.

22. Clapton, quoted in "Geldof, Bono 'Only Musicians,'" *Deutsch Presse-Agentur,* August 24, 2005.

23. "Do Dems Take Policy Points from Hollywood?" *O'Reilly Factor,* September 13, 2005. James Hirsen's provocative book is entitled, *Hollywood Nation: Left Coast Lies, Old Media Spin, and the New Media Revolution* (New York: Random House, 2005).

24. "Is Celebrity Charity Just Public Relations?" *The O'Reilly Factor,* June 28, 2006.

25. Bianca Jagger, "Real People Power, or Pernicious Platitudes?" *New Statesman,* July 11, 2005, 13.

CHAPTER 2

1. CNN advertises its program on the UN with Richard Roth, *Diplomatic License,* as a peek behind the closed doors of the organization.

2. Stuart Wavell, "Ambassador for Aid—Audrey Hepburn," *Guardian,* March 29, 1988. Tigre is still an Ethiopian province, but Eritrea became independent in 1993.

3. Ibid.

4. Ibid.

5. Hepburn, quoted in *Newsweek*, "UNICEF's Elegant Ambassador," April 4, 1988.

6. Hepburn, quoted in Associated Press, "Actress Audrey Hepburn Campaigns against World Hunger," April 14, 1988.

7. David Briscoe, "Audrey Hepburn Pleads with Congress for African Aid," Associated Press, June 4, 1991.

8. Hepburn, quoted in Alan Riding, "25 Years Later, Honor for Audrey Hepburn," *New York Times*, April 22, 1991.

9. Hepburn, quoted in Wavell, "Ambassador for Aid."

10. Hepburn, quoted in Didrikke Schanche, "Audrey Hepburn Describes Somalia as a 'Slice of Hell,'" Associated Press, September 24, 1992; Robert M. Press, "A Visit of Compassion to Somalia," *Christian Science Monitor*, October 5, 1992.

11. Moore, quoted in "Interview with Roger Moore," *Breakfast with Frost*, BBC, June 15, 2003.

12. Press, "A Visit of Compassion to Somalia."

13. Ullmann, quoted in Frank Sesno, "Women and Children Make Up 80 percent of World Refugees," CNN, February 8, 1993.

14. Loren, quoted in Philippe Naughton, "Sophia Loren Becomes Goodwill Ambassador for Refugees," Reuters, November 18, 1992.

15. Loren, quoted in *Toronto Star*, "Loren Shaken by First Sight of Starvation in Somalia," November 23, 1992.

16. *Associated Press*, "Actress Audrey Hepburn Campaigns."

17. Hepburn, quoted in David W. Jones, "Audrey Hepburn Urges Peace in Sudan," United Press International, April 17, 1989.

18. Gere, quoted in Abdul Latheef, "From Elizabeth Taylor to Madonna, from Gore Vidal to John Le Carré, Many Celebrities Are Voicing Their Frustration over Washington's Apparent Rush toward a War against Iraq," Canadian Press, February 15, 2003. Gere was booed off the stage at a concert in Madison Square Garden for the benefit of victims of the 9/11 attacks for advocating compassion in the face of aggression.

19. Ingo Gilmore, "Poll Plea to Muslims from Buddhist Gere," *Daily Telegraph*, January 6, 2005.

20. Gere, quoted in *Kitchener–Waterloo Record*, "Gere Slams China, UN over Tibet," April 27, 1999.

21. Sue Cameron, "Dressing Down a Princess," *Times*, April 5, 1996.

22. Princess Diana, quoted in Martin Bashir, "Queen of Hearts," *BBC Panorama*, November 20, 1995. Making headlines worldwide, she proclaimed of her relationship with Prince Charles, "There were three of us in this marriage, so it was a bit crowded" (referring to the prince's affair with Camilla Parker Bowles). In the same interview, she confessed to her own affair with James Hewitt, her riding instructor.

23. David Taylor, "All Eyes on Diana as She Takes the Envoy Test," *Evening Standard*, November 24, 1995.

24. UK official, quoted in Cameron, "Dressing Down a Princess."

25. Margarette Driscoll, "The Care Label," *Sunday Times*, May 2, 1993. Although given credit for her tangible achievements, most notably her delivery of a substantive amount of medical aid, Jagger was accused of being overbearing and a publicity hound.

26. Yad Luthra, quoted in Christina Lamb, "Minefield," *Sunday Times*, January 19, 1997. Interestingly, the Red Cross had debated the merits of using celebrities in crisis zones at the immediate end of the Cold War. Although admitting the awkwardness of such initiatives, the Red Cross had incentives to work out a plan along these lines. In the words of one

Red Cross official: "We are trying to build up a celebrity data base. People empathise with celebrities and in a disaster area … the publicity is vital. The aid workers may find it hard to tolerate stars but without their public support they wouldn't be there." The same official had earlier rejected out of hand the possibility of using Madonna as a celebrity ambassador, saying, "No, she would not be suitable." Colin McCallum, quoted in Alice Thompson: "It's the Fashion of Compassion," *Times,* July 30, 1993.

27. Ibid.

28. Princess Diana, quoted in Jerry White, "Travels with Diana: A Land-Mine Survivor's Tale," *Christian Science Monitor,* September 3, 1997.

29. Paul Eastham, "Blair's Mine Crusade in Diana's Memory," *Daily Mail,* October 2, 1997.

30. Princess Diana, quoted in "Tony Blair Offered Diana Role as Informal Ambassador," Agence France Presse, September 7, 1997.

31. Maureen Dowd, "Washington Is Star-Struck as Hollywood Gets Serious," *New York Times,* May 8, 1993. See also R. W. Apple Jr., "Hollywood, D.C.," *New York Times Magazine,* November 15, 1998. For part of the conservative backlash to this trend, see Michael Medved, "Hollywood's Contribution to Anti-Americanism Abroad," *National Interest* 68 (Summer 2002), 5–14.

32. Gere, quoted in Kim Bielenberg, "This week Nicole Kidman visited Kosovo as a UN goodwill ambassador, the latest celebrity to indulge in some 'charitainment' but is it all for the benefit of the stars themselves?" *Irish Independent,* October 17, 2006.

33. CNN, "Annan Courts Celebrity Support in L.A. Visit," April 22, 1998.

34. Mark D. Alleyne, "The United Nations' Celebrity Diplomacy," *SAIS Review* 25, no. 1 (Winter–Spring 2005), 176.

35. Annan, quoted in Agence France-Presse, "UN-Celebrities: Annan Says UN Goodwill Counteracts Cynicism," October 23, 2000. Ronald Mendoza, from the UNDP, adds, "to their credit, Bono and Angelina Jolie have probably done more to make the world aware of the Millennium Development Goals than most development experts." Ronald Mendoza, "You Don't Have to Be an Aid Expert to Make a Difference," *Financial Times,* February 3, 2006.

36. Sarah, Duchess of York, quoted in Richard Kay, "UN Ambassador Fergie: I Won't Be Simply a Letterhead, Says the Royal Roving Envoy," *Daily Mail,* June 11, 1993.

37. Halliwell, quoted in James Barron, "Hey, Like They're on a Mission for the UN," *New York Times,* October 25, 1998.

38. Roz Paterson, "The UN-Used Ambassador: Former Spice Girl Disappears Without Trace," *Daily Record,* October 11, 1999.

39. Barron, "Hey, Like They're on a Mission for the UN."

40. Damien Cave, "Seeking Hollywood Endings to Global Problems," *New York Times,* September 25, 2005.

41. Ibid.

42. National Press Club Newsmaker Luncheon with Angelina Jolie, Goodwill Ambassador, United Nations Refugee Program, National Press Club, Washington, DC, March 8, 2005. It is important to add that Jolie initiated the "audition" process. In her words, "I called and said … 'I'm an actress … I don't want to go with the press. I just—if you could give me access, allow me on a trip so I could just witness and learn,' and they did and that was the beginning." Jolie, quoted in Scott Simon, "Angelina Jolie Discusses Her Work with the United Nations High Commissioner for Refugees," National Public Radio, October 25, 2003.

43. Annan spokesman, quoted in Vivek Chaudhary, "The UN Can't Do It. Nor Can the Pope. Now Its Sven and Nancy's Turn to Try for World Peace," *Guardian*, September 15, 2003.

44. Bellamy, quoted in Anita Singh, "Goodwill Ambassador Beckham to Appeal over Tsunami Children," Press Association, January 12, 2005.

45. Matt Driscoll, "It Was Becks Wot Won It," *News of the World*, July 10, 2005.

46. Oliver Burkeman, "Ted's Tears," *Guardian*, June 18, 2002.

47. Dianne Sawyer, "Jolie, Damon, and DeNiro: The Good Shepherds," *20/20—ABC News* transcripts, December 15, 2006.

48. Richard Roth, "Interview with Angelina Jolie," *CNN International*, June 22, 2005.

49. UN spokesperson, quoted in Laura Barton, "What Is the Point of a UN Goodwill Envoy?" *Guardian*, November 25, 2005.

50. *BBC News*, "Jolie Given Cambodian Citizenship," August 12, 2005.

51. Jolie published the memoirs from her journeys to Sierra Leone, Tanzania, Pakistan, Cambodia, and Ecuador in her role as goodwill ambassador. In the book, she details her personal reaction to witnessing human suffering in refugee camps and shares her motivations for humanitarian activity. Angelina Jolie, *Notes from My Travels* (New York: Pocket Books, 2003).

52. *Daily Telegraph*, "After Tony and Kofi Fail, Brad and Jennifer Try Mid-East Diplomacy," October 26, 2003.

53. On this relationship, see Alex Blimes, "Sachs Appeal," *Spectator*, May 14, 2005. Bono, it needs to be added, wrote the foreword to *The End of Poverty*, the book that attracted Angelina Jolie's attention to Sachs.

54. Jonathan Curiel, "Star Power: When Celebrities Support Causes, Who Really Winds Up Benefiting?" *San Francisco Chronicle*, June 5, 2005. For this activity, Gabriel won the Man of Peace 2006 award at the annual summit of Nobel Peace prize laureates by the Gorbachev Foundation and the City of Rome. See http://www.witness.org.

CHAPTER 3

1. Ann Florini, *The Coming Democracy: New Rules for Running a New World* (Washington, DC: Brookings Institution Press, 2005), 166.

2. Edith M. Lederer, "Media Mogul Ted Turner Plans to Spend $500 Million in Next 10 Years on UN—and Hopefully Replenish His Fortune as Well," Associated Press, December 11, 2002.

3. James Traub, "The Statesman: Why, and How, Bono Matters," *New York Times Magazine*, September 18, 2005, 80.

4. Bush, quoted in Madeleine Bunting and Oliver Burkeman, "Pro Bono," *Guardian*, March 18, 2002, G2. See also Sebastian Mallaby, "Pro Bono," *Washington Post*, September 25, 2000, A21.

5. Durbin, quoted in Donna Cassata, "Bono Doubles as Lobbyist for World's Poor," Associated Press, June 7, 2005.

6. See the now archived website for the yet-unpublished book, *Bono the Puppet*, http://web.archive.org/web/20040826104052/www.bonothepuppet.com/why.htm (accessed April 11, 2007).

7. Bono, quoted in Sylvia Patterson, "Pop Smart," *Sunday Herald,* November 5, 2000, 7.

8. Bono, quoted in Chrissy Iley, "The Luck of the Irish," *Sunday Times,* February 25, 2001.

9. Bono, quoted in "Catholic Guilt behind Bono's Charity Work," *Belfast News,* November 24, 2000, 13.

10. Bono, quoted in Claire Donnelly, "Bono Puts Pope in the Shade: He Hands Pontiff His Sunglasses," *Mirror,* September 24, 1999.

11. Bono, quoted in Richie Taylor, "I'm Praying Heaven's for Real: U2 Star Reveals His Faith," *People,* October 16, 2005. For a thorough account of this movement, see Elizabeth A. Donnelly, "Proclaiming Jubilee: The Debt and Structural Adjustment Network," in Sanjeev Khagram, James V. Riker, and Kathryn Sikkink, eds., *Restructuring World Politics: Transnational Social Movements, Networks, and Norms* (Minneapolis: University of Minnesota Press, 2002), 155–180.

12. On this type of personal background, see Michka Assayas, *Bono in Conversation with Michka Assayas* (London: Riverhead Penguin, 2005).

13. Bunting and Burkeman, "Pro Bono."

14. Bono, quoted in Gerry Smyth, "Show Me the Way to Go Home: Space and Place in the Music of U2," in *Space and the Irish Imagination* (New York: Palgrave, 2001), 200.

15. Bono, quoted in John Deane, "Bono Plea to Blair and Brown over Africa," Press Association, September 29, 2004.

16. Bono, quoted in Victoria Ward, "Bono Attacks EU over Broken Aid Pledges," Press Association, June 1, 2004.

17. Bono, quoted in Geoff Meade, "People Don't Share EU Vision—Bono," Press Association, June 9, 2005.

18. For the context of Bono's activist turn, see Robin Denselow, *When the Music's Over: The Story of Political Pop* (London: Faber and Faber, 1990), 168, 259. Inspired by his involvement with Amnesty International, Bono visited Nicaragua and El Salvador in the mid-1980s. What are usually deemed to be his most political songs—"Bullet the Blue Sky" and "Mothers of the Disappeared"—are contained in the U2's *The Joshua Tree.*

19. Bono, quoted in Greg Kot, "How U2's Front Worked Washington's Back Channels (and Made Jesse Helms Cry) to Push Third World Debt Relief," *Rolling Stone,* December 28, 2000.

20. Bono, quoted in Sheryl Gay Stolberg, "A Calling to Heal: Getting Religion on AIDS," *New York Times,* February 2, 2003, Section 4, 1.

21. Bono, quoted in Neil McCormick, "Bob and Bono's Excellent Adventure," *Daily Telegraph,* July 2, 2005, 021.

22. Bono, quoted in David Robson, "What every politician needs is a friend in Rock N' Roll," *Express,* October 2, 2004.

23. Andrew Collier, "How Ali and Bono Do Better Than Geldof," *Scottish Daily Record,* February 18, 1999.

24. Bono, quoted in "Even I Get Sick of Bono," *Daily Mail (London),* May 21, 2007, 19.

25. The Edge, quoted in Chrissy Iley, "U2 Interview: Group Therapy," *Sunday Times,* November 7, 2004.

26. Greg Kot, "Bono's Victory," *Rolling Stone,* December 28, 2000.

27. Bono embellished the story of their meeting: "[When] I said I was from U2 he had flashbacks from Cuba, 1962." In his memorable address to the Harvard graduating class,

Bono made fun of Summers's about face: "If you're called up before the [then] new president of Harvard and he gives you the hairy eyeball, drums his fingers and generally acts disinterested, it could be the beginning of a great adventure." He is quoted in *Catholic New Times*, "Bono Rocks the Jubilee," September 9, 2001.

28. Bono, quoted in Bunting and Burkeman, "Pro Bono."

29. Bono, quoted in Jon Craig, "You Two Are a Credit, PM Tells Pop Star Debt-Busters," *Sunday Express*, January 21, 2001.

30. Bono, quoted in *Economist*, "Pro Bono: Foreign Aid," November 5, 2005.

31. Bono, quoted in John Deane, "Bono Plea to Blair."

32. Helms's aide, quoted in Bill Boles, "Helm's Reversal on AIDS Reverberates," *Boston Globe*, March 27, 2002, A12.

33. See Faye Fiore and Adam Schreck, "Washington Sexual Fantasy Service 'Madam' Identifying Clients," *Los Angeles Times*, May 1, 2007.

34. DATA official, quoted in Eamon Jarvis, "Bono's K Street Connection," *Vantage Point*, March 28, 2005.

35. On the power of voice more generally in international relations, see Anna Holzcheiter, "Discourse as Capability: Non-State Actors' Capital in Global Governance," *Millennium* 33, no. 3 (August 2005): 745.

36. Bush quoted in "'Bono for President' Says Bush as Stars Come Out for G8," *Irish Independent*, June 7, 2007.

37. Caroline Bock, "Celebrities Join Anti-poverty Protests," Deutsche Presse-Agentur, June 1, 2007.

38. Bono, quoted in McCormick, "Bob and Bono's Excellent Adventure."

39. BBC News, "'Get Real' on Africa, Urges Bono," September 29, 2004, http://news.bbc.co.uk/2/hi/uk_news/politics/3699234.stm (accessed April 11, 2007).

40. Iley, "U2 Interview: Group Therapy."

41. Bono, quoted in Stolberg, "A Calling to Heal."

42. Bono abundantly repaid this intellectual debt. Before the Harvard graduates he warmly praised this source of inspiration: "Jeffrey Sachs not only let me into his office, he let me into his Rolodex, his head and life." Bono also wrote the preface to Sachs's best-seller, *The End of Poverty*.

43. Bono, quoted in Farah Khan, "Bono Hopes Trip Will Loosen U.S. Purse Strings," IPS Service, May 24, 2002.

44. Bono quoting Powell's words in Ju-Lin Tan, "Bono and Bob Urge Blair to Take Lead in AIDS Battle," Press Association, May 22, 2003.

45. Bono, quoted in Traub, "The Statesman," 86.

46. Bono, quoted in Richard W. Stevenson, "Accra Journal: No Mosh Pit, This, But Some Enthusiasm for Aid," *New York Times*, May 22, 2002, A4.

47. Bono, quoted in Kevin Ward, "Rock Star Praises Martin for Stance on Debt Relief," *Toronto Star*, September 26, 2000.

48. Bono, quoted in Jeff Sallot, "Bono 'Crushed' by PM's Failure on Foreign Aid," *Globe and Mail*, November 26, 2005.

49. Paul Krugman, "Heart of Cheapness," *New York Times*, May 31, 2002, 23.

50. Bono, quoted in Deane, "Bono Plea to Blair and Brown."

51. Angela Pacienza, "Alicia Keys Says Mixing Music, Politics Natural but 'Time Consuming,'" Canadian Press, September 29, 2005. Alicia Keys subsequently set up her own organization, Keep a Child Alive, which established family care clinics focused on patients with HIV/AIDS.

52. Andrew F. Cooper, John English, and Ramesh Thakur, *Enhancing Global Governance: Towards a New Diplomacy?* (Tokyo: United Nations University Press, 2002).

53. Jane Cowan, "Bono Discusses Foreign Aid with Costello," *Australian Broadcasting Corporation Transcripts,* November 20, 2006.

54. Matthew d'Ancona, "Mr. Blair Tunes Up for His Gleneagles Gig," *Daily Telegraph,* July 3, 2005.

CHAPTER 4

1. On the primacy of ambiguity in diplomatic practice, see the classic account by Sir Ernest Satow, *A Guide to Diplomatic Practice,* 2nd ed. (London: Longman, 1922).

2. Geldof, quoted in David Thomas, "The many trials of St. Bob," *Sunday Telegraph,* May 22, 2005.

3. Ali Hewson's public profile increased with the launch of her Edun fashion label in 2004. The best-known product line of Edun is a promotional T-shirt for ONE: The Campaign to Make Poverty History.

4. Geldof, quoted in Paul Vallely, "All He Wants Now Is a Life to Call His Own," *Independent,* July 15, 1995.

5. Jasper Gerard, "Handbuilt for the Driven Man," *Sunday Times,* June 26, 2005.

6. Rachel Williams, "Geldof Tired of the Politics of Being Nice," Press Association, February 3, 2005.

7. Geldof, quoted in Roy Carroll, "The G8 Summit: The Campaigner," *Observer,* June 1, 2003.

8. Geldof, quoted in "Rock Star Blasts UN Session for Africa," *Associated Press,* May 29, 1986.

9. Geldof, quoted in Jill Rowbotham, "The Moral Entrepreneur," *Courier-Mail* (Brisbane), August 2, 1986.

10. "Cutting the frills for Geldof," *Guardian,* October 21, 1985.

11. Nigel Nelson, "Geldof takes Blair to Africa," *People,* August 1, 2004.

12. Geldof, quoted in Paul Vallely, "Geldof: 'I Don't Want Our Image of the Future to Be Children Dying on TV'," *Independent,* February 27, 2004. For detailed contextual analysis, see Ramesh Thakur, Andrew F. Cooper, and John English, eds., *International Commissions and the Power of Ideas* (Tokyo: United Nations University Press, 2005).

13. Geldof, quoted in Chris Hughes and Kate Thornton, "I Went to Ethiopia to Escape Paula," *Daily Mirror,* July 11, 1995.

14. Paul Vallely, "It Is 17 Years Since Live Aid and Bob Geldof Is Back, Telling the World to Listen to Africa," *Independent,* May 13, 2002.

15. "Geldof Slams West over Africa AIDS and Famine Fear," *Mirror,* June 2, 2003.

16. Ure, quoted in Owen Gibson and Sandra Laville, "Live 8: Old White Guys Singing the Wrong Tune?" *Guardian,* June 4, 2005.

17. For one critical assessment of these connections, see Geoffrey Wansell, "Saint Bob Exposed," *Daily Mail,* June 7, 2003. For another assessment, see Raymond Snoddy, "A New Frontier for Planet Bob," *Independent,* April 10, 2006.

18. Geldof, quoted in Peter Aspden, "Songwriting, Sainthood and Masterly Swearing," *Financial Times,* November 1, 2005.

19. Paul Redfern, "Britain to Push for Africa's Debt Relief," *Nation* (Kenya), December 10, 2004.

20. Blair, quoted in Pippa Crerar, "Bob's Amazing Rant," *Daily Record,* March 12, 2005.

21. Brown, quoted in Hannah K. Strange, "Blair and Bush Head for G8 Clash," United Press International, June 6, 2005.

22. See David Kertzer, *Ritual, Power, and Politics* (New Haven, CT: Yale University Press, 1988), 104.

23. Geldof, quoted in Vallely, "It Is 17 Years since Live Aid."

24. Brauman, quoted in Richard Beeston, "Geldof the Gullible?" *Times,* November 9, 2000.

25. Ure, quoted in John Burns and Allan Brown, "Ure 'Stabbed in the Back' by Geldof's People at Live Aid," *Sunday Times,* October 10, 2004. See also John Meager, "Live 8: Battle of the Egos," *Irish Independent,* July 2, 2005.

26. Simms, quoted in Charlotte Denny, "Do Celebrities Hurt the Cause?" *Manchester Guardian Weekly,* March 20, 2002.

27. For one scathing attack on this approach see Katharine Quarmby, "Why Oxfam Is Failing Africa," *New Statesman,* May 30, 2005.

28. Raymond Whitaker, "Geldof's Praise for the U.S. Is Criticized by Aid Agencies," *Independent,* May 29, 2003.

29. "Geldof Slams West over Africa," *Mirror.*

30. Anthony Mitchell, "Geldof Calls on Africa to Throw Out Mugabe," *Times,* May 28, 2003.

31. See, for example, the comments by John O'Shea, chief executive of the international aid NGO, Goal, quoted in Gibson and Laville, "Live 8: Old White Guys Singing the Wrong Tune?"

32. Klu, quoted in George Monbiot, "And Still He Stays Quiet," *Guardian,* September 6, 2005. After some delay Geldof set out his defense, "What Did 2005 Achieve for Africa?" *Guardian,* December 28, 2005, G2.

33. "Pop Campaign on Africa Fizzles Out," *Inter-Press Service,* July 11, 2005.

34. The ambivalence Oxfam felt toward Geldof is captured by its paper on outcomes from the summit. Geldof was not mentioned by name in the document. The tone of the assessment tried to capture the middle ground between Geldof's positive perspective and the negativity expressed by much of the rest of civil society: "No previous G8 summit has done as much for development, particularly in Africa. However, along with other organisations and fellow campaigners, Oxfam is disappointed that in the light of undisputed need and unprecedented popular pressure and expectation, neither the necessary sense of urgency nor the historic potential of Gleneagles was grasped by the G8." Max Lawson and Duncan Green, "Gleneagles: What Really Happened at the G8 Summit?" *Oxfam,* July 29, 2005.

35. On this theme, see Gary Younge, "New Beat to Saving the World from Debt," *Guardian,* February 15, 1999.

36. Stephen Lewis, *Race against Time: Searching for Hope in AIDS-Ravaged Africa,* 2nd ed. (Toronto: House of Anansi, 2006), 26.

CHAPTER 5

1. Samuel P. Huntington, *The Clash of Civilizations and the Remaking of World Order* (New York: Simon and Schuster, 1996).

2. "In Praise of Davos Man: How Businessmen May Accidentally Be Making the World Safer," *Economist,* February 1, 1997.

3. Shaun Riordan, *The New Diplomacy: Themes for the Twenty-First Century* (Cambridge: Polity, 2002), 1. The *Economist* had long shared this view, arguing that space should be freed up beyond "the stuffier members of the diplomats' trade union.... The freelancers are coming. The diplomats should open their closed door." See "Privatized Diplomacy," *Economist*, February 15, 1986.

4. William Keegan, "Summit Hope for a Pro-Bono Gesture," *Observer*, January 30, 2005, 8.

5. Paul Krugman, "Davos Man Needs to Resolve an Image Problem," *International Herald Tribune*, January 24, 2000.

6. John Ralston Saul, *The Collapse of Globalism and the Reinvention of the World* (Toronto: Viking Canada, 2005), 66.

7. Sasha Frere Jones, "Schmooze Operators: Inside the World Economic Forum," *Village Voice*, February 5, 2002.

8. Mark Landler, "Guess Who's Coming to Davos," *New York Times*, January 20, 2005, C1.

9. On the element of theater in diplomacy, see Raymond Cohen, *Theatre of Power: The Art of Diplomatic Signaling* (London: Longman, 1997).

10. Peres, quoted in Landler, "Guess Who's Coming to Davos."

11. Saul, *The Collapse of Globalism.*

12. Evans, quoted in Anthony Browne, "Meeting of Minds Can Turn Talk into Action," *Times* [London], January 31, 2005, 30.

13. For details, see Geoffrey Allen Pigman, *The World Economic Forum: A Multi-Stakeholder Approach to Global Governance* (New York: Routledge, 2006), 24.

14. Thomas Friedman, *The World Is Flat: A Brief History of the Twenty-first Century* (New York: Farrar, Straus, and Giroux, 2005).

15. Kissinger, quoted in Richard Roeper, "What's a Good Looking Gal Doing with a Guy Like This?" *Chicago Sun-Times*, May 25, 1997. See also Walter Isaacson, "Celebrity," in *Kissinger* (New York: Simon and Schuster, 1992), chap. 17.

16. Sorrell, quoted in Eric Pfanner, "Leaders in Davos Are Hoping for More Than Just a Talkfest," *International Herald Tribune*, January 21, 2004.

17. Maathai, quoted in Browne, "Meeting of Minds."

18. Jeff Faux, "The Party of Davos," *Nation*, February 13, 2006.

19. Gareth Harding, "Hollywood in the Alps," United Press International, January 29, 2005.

20. Jay Nordlinger, "In Davos, Part 1," *Impromptus*, January 27, 2005, http://www.nationalreview.com/impromptus/impromptus200501270744.asp (accessed April 11, 2007). Davos has an official blog: http://www.forumblog.org. There are also a number of blogs devoted specially to Davos including http://www.davosnewbies.com; http://www.ft.com/davosforum; and http://opendemocracy.typepad.com/davos.

21. Timothy L. O'Brien, "Can Angelina Jolie Really Save the World?" *New York Times*, January 30, 2005.

22. BBC News, "Actress Stone Raises Fast Million," January 29, 2005. Stone, quoted in Harding, "Hollywood in the Alps." The theatrical element was enhanced by the presence of Angelina Jolie and Richard Gere in the audience.

23. Kevin G. Hall, "When Stars Converge, Stodgy Forum Perks Up," Knight Ridder News Service, January 30, 2005.

24. O'Brien, "Can Angelina Jolie Really Save the World?"

25. Harding, "Hollywood in the Alps."

26. Bono, quoted in Nick Robinson, "Four Brainy White Men Who Know That African Poverty Is Stupid," *Times* (London), January 29, 2005.

27. *Canberra Times,* "Bono Tunes in to 'Punk Rock' Commerce in Renewed Fight against Poverty," February 4, 2006.

28. See Gates Foundation. "Advocacy—Grants," http://www.gatesfoundation.org/globalhealth/otherinitiatives/advocacy/grants/grant-28711.htm (accessed April 11, 2007).

29. *CNN Larry King Weekend,* "Interview with Bono," December 1, 2002.

30. Melinda Gates, quoted in Josh Tyangiel, "The Constant Charmer," *Time,* December 19, 2005; Josh Tyangiel, "We Just Go Off," *Time,* December 19, 2005.

31. John Authers, "Interview with George Soros," March 20, 2002, http://www.geocities.com/ecocorner/intelarea/gs20.html (accessed April 11, 2007).

32. Francesco Guerrera and Sundeep Tucker, "Jet-Set Diplomacy Forges Strong Ties with China," *Financial Times,* June 1, 2006.

33. George Pitcher, "Can a Young Bill Succeed Where Uncle Sam Failed," *Marketing Week,* February 3, 2005.

34. Landler, "Guess Who's Coming to Davos."

35. For the contradictory elements in Soros's character, see Jeffrey A. Frankel, "Soros's Split Personality," *Foreign Affairs* 78, no. 2 (March–April 1999): 124–130.

36. See "Asia's Financial Crisis, 1997–1999," *Washington Post,* Asian Economies Report, 1998, http://www.washingtonpost.com/wp-srv/business/longterm/asiaecon/timeline.htm (accessed April 11, 2007).

37. George Soros, Arthur Harman, and Wesley Clark, "Bush Policies on Iraq and the War on Terror," News Conference, National Press Club, Washington, D.C., September 28, 2004.

38. Peter Singer, "What Should a Billionaire Give—and What Should You?" *New York Times,* December 17, 2006, Sec. 6, 58.

39. "Bill Gates Slams Govts and Industry over Poverty Funding 'Failure,'" *Pharma Marketletter,* January 31, 2001.

40. John Heilemann, "The Softening of a Software Man," *New York Times Magazine,* January 3, 2006.

41. Bono, quoted in Michael Specter, "What Money Can Buy: Millions of Africans Die Needlessly of Disease Each Year. Can Bill Gates Change That?" *New Yorker,* October 24, 2005.

42. Floyd Norris, "George Soros Backs Obama (But Hedges His Bets)," *New York Times,* January 27, 2007.

43. The International Renaissance Foundation spent $15,078,000 in the Ukraine between 2002 and 2004. See Soros Foundations Networks, "Building Open Societies," 2002 Report, Open Societies Institute, 2003; Soros Foundations Networks, "Building Open Societies," 2003 Report, Open Societies Institute, 2004.

44. Gates, quoted in Specter, "What Money Can Buy."

45. This contribution amounted to about half of GAVI's resources, although the alliance itself was made up of UN agencies, corporate representatives, and a set of national governments. See "Global Health: The World's Richest Charity Confronts the Health of the World's Poorest People," *Economist,* January 29, 2005, 84.

46. Morton Abramowitz and Michael T. Kaufman, *Soros: The Life and Times of a Messianic Billionaire* (New York: Knopf, 2002), 290.

47. Andrew Jack, "Gates and Brown Back New Global War on TB," *Financial Times,* January 28, 2006.

48. Malloch Brown, quoted in Danna Harman, "Mr. Soros Goes to Washington," *Christian Science Monitor,* August 25, 2004. Kaufman notes that both Malloch Brown and Abramowitz were "allies and advisors" to Soros. He also adds that Soros hired a former State Department official (John Fox) to serve as an "ambassador," operating out of the OSI office in Washington, D.C. Kaufman, *Soros,* 292.

49. This negative image was compounded by charges that the Gates Foundation had been involved in unethical investment practices that contradict the organization's purpose. Charles Piller, "Money Clashes with Mission," *Los Angeles Times,* January 8, 2007.

50. Andrew Jack, "Gates Learns That Even in Charity There Can Be Controversy," *Financial Times,* June 13, 2006.

51. Jens Martens, "Multistakeholders Partnerships—Future Models of Multilateralism?" Dialogue on Globalization Occasional Papers, Friedrich Ebert Stiftung, Berlin, No. 29, January 2007, 41.

52. Neil Clark, "NS Profile: George Soros," *New Statesman,* June 2, 2003. See also: Leigh Phillips, "Sugar Daddies and Revolutions," *New Statesman,* December 8, 2003.

53. Malloch Brown, quoted in Harman, "Mr. Soros Goes to Washington."

54. The role of Melinda Gates—like that of Ali Hewson—deserves more attention. She is often termed the "most powerful woman you know next to nothing about." Clayton Collins, "Behind the Golden Gates," *Christian Science Monitor,* July 31, 2006.

55. Andrew Jack, "The Casual-Trousered Philanthropists: The Bill and Melinda Gates Foundation Is the World's Largest Charity and Spends More Each Year on Health and Education Than the World Health Organization," *Financial Times,* March 11, 2006.

56. Steven Pearlstein, "Sending My Regrets and My Doubts," *Washington Post,* January 26, 2005.

57. Bello, quoted in Tony Smith, "Davos and Porto Alegre Link Up and Fight It Out," *Associated Press,* January 29, 2001.

58. Alan Beattie, "Plan for Globalization Debate Finds Antagonists Poles Apart," *Financial Times,* August 21, 2001. The "Davos" panel was in fact quite diverse, consisting of Soros, Mark Malloch Brown, John Ruggie, and the head of communications for the Swedish-Swiss multinational ABB, a strong supporter of the corporate social responsibility initiative.

59. Immanuel Wallerstein, "The Rising Strength of the World Social Forum," *World Social Forum,* February 20, 2004, as quoted in Peter Smith, "The World Social Forum—a New Space of Politics?" Paper presented at the Annual Meeting of the Canadian Political Science Association, Winnipeg, June 3–5, 2004. Naomi Klein is equally scathing about the WSF's tilt toward bigness, whether big speeches or big men. Naomi Klein, "Cut the Strings," *Guardian,* February 1, 2003.

60. Clinton, quoted in Sarah Baxter, "The Comeback Kid Isn't Finished," *Sunday Times,* August 7, 2005. See also Pranay Gupte, "A Clinton Duel against Davos Is in the Offing," *New York Sun,* August 4, 2005.

61. The leadership ambitions of the Clinton Foundation stood out as well through its hosting role of a recent summit on philanthropy in Little Rock, Arkansas. Jacob Weisberg, "Rise of the competitive philanthropists," *Financial Times,* November 15, 2006.

62. BBC News, "Branson Makes $3bn Climate Pledge," September 21, 2006, http://news.bbc.co.uk/1/hi/business/5368194.stm (accessed April 11, 2007).

63. *The Business,* "Drivel in Business," January 30, 2005.

64. Andrew Gowers, "Davos: Beanfeast of Pomp and Platitude," *Sunday Times,* January 22, 2006.

65. Schwab, quoted in Mark Landler, "Reworking the A-List; Those Invited to Davos Reflect This Year's Theme of a Shift in Power," *New York Times,* April 3, 2007.

66. Bryan Appleyard, "The Most Powerful Circuit in the World," *Independent,* January 31, 1995.

67. Schwab, quoted in Andrew Ross Sorkin, "No Frivolity: Davos Tries Fewer Stars," *New York Times,* January 26, 2007.

CHAPTER 6

1. On the notion of cosmopolitan citizenship, see David Held, *Democracy and the Global Order: From the Modern State to Cosmopolitan Governance* (Cambridge and Palo Alto: Polity and Stanford University Press, 1995).

2. Lyrics played at Live 8. Quoted in Jamie Doward, "We Don't Want Charity, What We Want Is Justice," *Observer,* July 3, 2005. The correct lyrics are, "We get to carry each other."

3. See the debate around these exclusionary practices: Andy Kershaw, "The Live 8 Controversy: Africans Not Included," *Independent,* June 4, 2005; Patrick Barkham, "Discord behind the Harmonies for Artists Who Felt Snubbed," *Guardian,* July 4, 2005.

4. DATA's board of directors includes Bono, Susie Buffett (the oldest daughter of Warren Buffett), Jamie Drummond, Bobby Shriver, Morton H. Halperin (director of U.S. advocacy at the Open Society Institute), and Patty Stonesifer (the CEO of the Bill and Melinda Gates Foundation).

5. "Stars Quit Charity in Corruption Scandal," *Guardian,* January 11, 2001.

6. "Pro-Palestinian Demonstrators Picket Concert by Singer-for-Peace," Agence France Presse, November 26, 2000.

7. Macias, quoted in "I am a Singer, Not Don Quixote or a Hero," Agence France Presse, March 6, 2000.

8. Cataldi, quoted in "Glamour in a Good Cause," *Japan Times,* October 29, 2000.

9. Konno, quoted in "UNDP Envoy Urges International Help for Palestinians," Japan Economic Newswire, July 25, 2000.

10. David Nason, "Nicole, as UN Envoy, Is Mum on Abortion," *Weekend Australian,* January 28, 2006. This disinclination to court controversy has been marred by at least one journalistic attempt to fuel a rift between Kidman and Angelina Jolie. But that story was quickly retracted.

11. Hugh Williamson, "Geldof and Bono Take G8 Campaign to Germany," *Financial Times,* December 27, 2006.

12. Schiffer, quoted in Matt Bendoris, "Gleneagles, Are You Listening?" *Sun,* July 7, 2005.

13. For one critical account of Kouchner's role in Kosovo, see Michael Ignatieff, *Empire Lite: Nation-Building in Bosnia, Kosovo, and Afghanistan* (Toronto: Penguin, 2003): 45–75.

14. John Vinocur, "One Popular French Voice Who Supports a War," *International Herald Tribune,* February 26, 2003.

15. N'Dour, quoted in Giles Hattersley, "Singing for Africa's Supper," *Sunday Times*, August 28, 2005.

16. Hattersley, "Singing for Africa's Supper."

17. "Mandela Addresses Live 8 finale," *BBC News*, July 7, 2005.

18. "Saving Africa without Africans?" *Zimbabwe Standard*, July 10, 2005. See also Jean-Claude Shanda Tonme, "All Rock, No Action," *New York Times*, July 15, 2005 (reprinted from *Le Messager*, Cameroon).

19. Gabriel, quoted in Cole Moreton, "Live 8: Great Music, Massive Crowds, but Was Anybody Listening?" *Independent on Sunday*, July 3, 2005.

20. "Inside Africa, African Musicians Speak Out against Global Poverty," *CNN International News*, July 3, 2005.

21. James McNair, "World Music: The Goodwill Ambassador," *Independent*, June 18, 2004.

22. Michael Peel and David White, "Bridging the Social Divide? Profile: Youssou N'Dour," *Financial Times*, February 2, 2005.

23. Kidjo, quoted in "Inside Africa, African Musicians Speak Out against Global Poverty," *CNN International News*, July 3, 2005.

24. Maal, quoted in ibid.

25. Robin Denselow, "Voice of the People," *Guardian*, December 24, 2004.

26. Rose Skelton, "Rappers Rhyme for Change in Senegal," *Reuters*, August 2, 2005. See also Kevin Lock, "Who Is Listening? Hip-Hop in Sierra Leone, Liberia, and Senegal," in M. I. Franklin, ed., *Resounding International Relations: On Music, Culture, and Politics* (New York: Palgrave, 2005), 150–155.

27. Deborah Horab, "The Legend of Umm Kulthum," Inter Pares Service, July 16, 1997.

28. *Deutsche-Presse-Agentur*, "Egypt's Film Festival Excludes Israel, Homosexuality," November 25, 1998.

29. Atlas, quoted in Burhan Wazir, "There's Geri, Ronaldo and Me: The UN Usually Chooses Big Stars for the Role of Goodwill Ambassador, Natacha Atlas Doesn't Quite Fit the Bill—Yet," *Observer*, June 3, 2001.

30. Fiona Sturges, "Open N'Dour," *Independent*, December 13, 2002.

31. Peel and White, "Bridging the Social Divide?" February 2, 2005.

32. Jim White, "Weah's New Goal Is to Turn Sporting Celebrity into Political Career," *Daily Telegraph*, August 27, 2005.

33. Arundhati Roy, *War Talk* (Cambridge, MA: South End, 2003).

34. Associated Press, "Belafonte Says Bush Is 'Greatest Terrorist in the World,' Praises Venezuelan Dictator," January 6, 2006.

35. Lloyd Grove with Katherine Thompson, "Hillary's Not Wild about Harry," *New York Daily News*, January 13, 2006.

36. Ronald Radosh, "The Truth about UNICEF's Goodwill Ambassador," *New York Sun*, January 31, 2006.

37. "UNICEF Signs Amitabh Bachchan as Goodwill Ambassador," Press Trust of India, April 15, 2005.

38. Bachchan, quoted in "Films Can Help Bring India, Pakistan Closer: Bachchan," Press Trust of India, May 16, 2005.

39. John Pilger, "The Ghost at Gleneagles," *New Statesman*, July 11, 2005.

40. Ken Wiwa, "Listen to the Real Africa," *Observer*, July 3, 2005.

41. Brendan O'Neil, "Brad, Angelina and the Rise of 'Celebrity Colonialism,'" *Spiked,* May 30, 2006.

CONCLUSION

1. Kevin McDonald, *Global Movements: Action and Culture* (Oxford: Blackwell, 2006): 81–83. For the role of "personal subjects" more generally, see Alain Touraine, *Can We Live Together? Equality and Difference* (Stanford: Stanford University Press, 2000): 304.

2. George Haynal, "DOA: Diplomacy on the Ascendant in the Age of Disinterme-diation," *Fellows' Papers* (Cambridge, MA: Weatherhead Center for International Affairs, 2001–2002). Available online at http://www.wcfia.harvard.edu/fellows/papers/2001-02/haynal.pdf (accessed April 11, 2007).

3. Gordon S. Smith and Alan Sutherland, "The New Diplomacy: Real-Time Implications and Applications," in Evan H. Potter, ed., *Cyber Diplomacy; Managing Foreign Policy in the Twenty-First Century* (Montreal and Kingston: McGill and Queen's University Press, 2002), 158.

4. UNICEF head of celebrity relations, quoted in Peter Ford and Gloria Goodale, "Why Stars and Charities Need Each Other," *Christian Science Monitor,* January 13, 2005. This view has been echoed by the president of UNICEF UK, the eminent film producer, Lord David Puttnam: "Just scan the newsagent's magazine rack and you quickly see why the influence of celebrity has become an increasingly valuable currency." See "Lord David Puttnam Argues That the Behind-the-Scenes Work of Celebrities Is Vital to UNICEF's Success," *Guardian,* January 16, 2007.

5. Oxfam UK's head of advocacy, quoted in ibid. With this template in mind, Oxfam has shown a tremendous appetite for locating new celebrities to front their campaigns. To give just one illustration of this trend, Coldplay's Chris Martin has become Oxfam's most vocal "Make Trade Fair" spokesperson. Martin has appeared with Bono for "Make Trade Fair" and visited Haiti and Ghana for Oxfam.

6. Michael Fullilove, "Celebrities Should Concentrate on Their Day Jobs," *Financial Times,* February 1, 2006.

7. Ibid.

8. CNN People in the News, "Profile of Actress and U.N. Goodwill Ambassador Angelina Jolie," Interview with Paula Zahn, *CNN,* August 13, 2005.

9. Bob Strauss, "As Angelina Evolves, So Does Her 'Lara Croft' Character," *Daily News of Los Angeles,* July 25, 2003.

10. "Angelina Jolie: Her Mission and Motherhood," *Anderson Cooper 360°,* June 24, 2006.

11. Gareth Harding, "Hollywood in the Alps," United Press International, January 29, 2005. This sensitivity concerning the relationship between celebrities and front-line aid workers was at the core of the supposed remarks made by Nicole Kidman about Jolie, before Kidman embarked on her first official work with UNIFEM on a trip to India: "It's not like Angelina is any better than a nurse working in a hospital, but she's getting the publicity for her contributions." For the retraction, see *Scottish Daily Record,* "Nicole Kidman Apology," September 16, 2006.

12. Adan Elkus, "Celebrity Colonialism," *Colorlines* (March–April 2007).

13. "Jolie Adds Glamour to U.S. Think-Tank," *Financial Times,* February 26, 2007.

14. Nina Shea, "Clooney Does Darfur: If Only Our Politicians Were as Wise, Discerning, and Benevolent as George," *National Review Online,* May 2, 2006. Mark Steyn, in a similar vein, commented: "I wish the celebs well. Those of us who wanted action on Darfur years ago will hope their advocacy produces more results than ours did. Clooney's concern for the people of the region appears to be genuine and serious. But unless he's also serious about backing the only forces in the world with the capability and will to act in Sudan, he's just another showboating pretty boy of no use to anyone." Mark Steyn, "New Coalition of Willing Needed in Darfur," *Australian,* May 8, 2006.

15. See Don Cheadle and John Prendergast, *Not on Our Watch: The Mission to End Genocide in Darfur and Beyond* (New York: Hyperion, 2007). Associated with this book were luminaries such as Nobel Peace Prize winner and UN messenger of peace Elie Wiesel, who penned the foreword, and U.S. Senators Barrack Obama and Sam Brownback, who contributed the introduction.

16. Ronan Farrow and Mia Farrow, "Genocide Olympics," *Wall Street Journal,* March 28, 2007. See also Helene Cooper, "Darfur Collides with Olympics, and China Yields," *New York Times,* April 13, 2007.

17. See Andrew F. Cooper and Andrew Schrumm, "How Mia Farrow Got UN Troops into Darfur," *Embassy Newsweekly,* April 25, 2007, 1.

18. In an article that has otherwise spoofed the emergence of celebrity diplomats, Rob Long has accurately portrayed Bono's pivotal role. His core advice to other stars entering this arena was to "let Bono be your lodestar." Rob Long, "Using Your Star Power," *Foreign Policy,* no. 154 (May–June 2006): 74.

19. As might be expected, Geldof's escape from his association from New Labour did not free him from controversy. To his critics it was another sign that Geldof was not a celebrity who could be trusted. See, for example, Adrian Hamilton, "Geldof: Political Naivety or Just Plain Egotism?" *Independent,* December 30, 2005.

20. Bono and Geldof quoted in Benedict Brogan, "G8 Pledge a Disgrace Claim Bob and Bono," *Daily Mail (London),* June 9, 2007. For background, see Hugh Williamson, "Geldof and Bono Take G8 Campaign to Germany," *Financial Times,* December 27, 2006. DATA released its own compliance report just before the Heiligendamm summit. See http://www. thedatareport.org.

21. Peter Wahl quoted in Caroline Bock, "Celebrities Join Anti-poverty Protests," *Deutsche Presse-Agentur,* June 1, 2007.

22. Manuel Castells, *The Information Age: Economy, Society, and Culture,* vol. 3: *End of Millennium* (Oxford: Blackwell, 1998), 350.

23. Carol J. Loomis, "Warren Buffett Gives It All Away," *Fortune,* July 17, 2006; "Billanthropy: How to Spend Money and Influence People," *Economist,* July 1, 2006: 9. Reportedly, Bono was the first person Buffett phoned to tell about his extraordinary gift of over $31 billion to the Gates Foundation. Bono to Andy Serwer, CNN's *In the Money,* November 5, 2006, http://edition.cnn.com/TRANSCRIPTS/0611/04/cnnitm.01.html (accessed April 11, 2007). Buffett's expanding appetite for diplomacy can be witnessed by his recent pledge of $50 million for a international nuclear fuel bank—operated through the International Atomic Energy Agency—for states that chose not to establish nuclear reactors. See "Mr. Buffett's Excellent Idea," *New York Times,* September 28, 2006.

24. By its nature, it must be nuanced; this form of network is quite different from both the focused "government networks" highlighted by Anne-Marie Slaughter and the diffuse types of networks suggested by the work of Wolfgang Reinicke. Anne-Marie Slaughter, *A*

New World Order (Princeton, NJ: Princeton University Press, 2004); Wolfgang Reinicke, *Global Public Policy: Governing without Government?* (Washington, DC: Brookings Institution, 1998).

25. Bongani Madondo, "Lethal Weapon," *Sunday Times* (South Africa), November 7, 2004.

26. UNICEF, "Futbol Club Barcelona, UNICEF Team Up for Children in Global Partnership," September 7, 2006, http://www.unicef.org/media/media_35642.html (accessed April 11, 2007). Another Brazilian who demonstrates the range of celebrity diplomacy is Gilberto Gil, the internationally acclaimed musician, activist, and the minister of culture in President Lula's government.

27. Bill "Low-Key" Heinzelman, "Russell Simmons, Annan Urge African Aid to Double," *ALLHIPHOP NEWS*, July 4, 2005. Simmons himself became a UN goodwill ambassador in July 2006, as a member of the CISRI-ISP Permanent Mission (an intergovernmental organization that campaigns against hunger and malnutrition.

28. Sylvia Patterson, "Host with the Most," *Independent* (London), August 18, 2002.

29. Tom Moon, "Wyclef Jean's Jolt of Inspiration," *Philadelphia Inquirer,* August 20, 2000. This relationship had both an activist (via the Jubilee campaign) and musical (mutual admiration for the Fugees and U2) pillars. Anthony DeCurtis, "Think Globally, Act Musically," *Rolling Stone,* October 28, 1999.

30. Haiti Information Project, "It's Not All about That! Wyclef Is Fronting in Haiti," Commentary, *HaitiAction.net,* November 2, 2004.

31. Letta Tayler, "Home Is Where His Heart Is," *Newsday,* March 9, 2006.

32. Bono, quoted in Matthew Bishop, "View from Davos: Bono Marketing His Red Badge of Virtue View from Davos," *Daily Telegram,* January 27, 2006.

33. Leah Garchik, "Bono Takes His Place in the Cosmos," *San Francisco Chronicle,* February 2, 2002.

34. A breakdown of each product's donations is available at the Product Red website: http://www.joinred.com (accessed April 11, 2007).

35. Cahal Milmo, "Ethical Shopping: The Red Revolution," *Independent Online,* January 27, 2006. See also the (Red) edition of the *Independent*: Bono (guest editor), "I Am a Witness. What Can I Do?" *Independent,* May 16, 2006.

36. Richard Tomlinson and Fergal O'Brien, "Bono INC," *Bloomberg Markets,* March 2007, 69–77.

37. Lisa Ann Richey and Stefano Ponte, "Better (RED)™ Than Dead: 'Brand Aid,' Celebrities, and the New Frontier of Development Assistance," Danish Institute for International Studies Working Paper no. 26 (2006).

38. "Oprah and Bono Paint the Town Red," *Oprah Winfrey Show,* December 18, 2006.

39. "Aiming the Spotlight," *Cincinnati Post,* May 2, 2005.

40. John G. Ruggie, "Reconstituting the Global Public Domain: Issues, Actors, and Practices," *European Journal of International Relations* 10, no. 4 (December 2004): 519.

41. Mark Leonard and Liz Noble, "Being Public: How Diplomacy Will Need to Change to Cope with the Information Society," *iMP Magazine,* July 2001.

Acronyms

AIDS	acquired immunodeficiency syndrome
AMEX	American Express
BBC	British Broadcasting Corporation
CGI	Clinton Global Initiative
CIGI	Centre for International Governance Innovation
CNN	Cable News Network
DATA	Debt, AIDS, Trade, Africa
EU	European Union
G8	Group of Eight (Industrialized Nations)
G20	Group of Twenty (Finance Ministers Meeting)
GAVI	Global Alliance for Vaccines and Immunization
GHIs	global health initiatives
GNI	gross national income
HIV	human immunodeficiency virus
IOC	International Olympic Committee
MDGs	Millennium Development Goals
MSF	Médecins sans Frontières
MTV	Music Television
NATO	North Atlantic Treaty Organization
NGOs	non-governmental organizations
NRA	National Rifle Association
ODA	Official Development Assistance
OSI	Open Society Institute
TB	tuberculosis
UK	United Kingdom
UN	United Nations
UNDP	United Nations Development Programme
UNFPA	United Nations Population Fund
UNHCR	United Nations High Commissioner for Refugees
UNHRC	United Nations Human Rights Commission
UNICEF	United Nations Children's Fund
UNIFEM	United Nations Development Fund for Women
USAID	United States Agency for International Development
WEF	World Economic Forum
WHO	World Health Organization
WSF	World Social Forum
WTO	World Trade Organization

Index

 Mark A. Boyer, University of Connecticut, Series Editor

Editorial Board

Robin Broad, *American University*

Michael Butler, *Clark University*

Dan Caldwell, *Pepperdine University*

Mary Caprioli, *University of Minnesota, Duluth*

Robert Denemark, *University of Delaware*

A. Cooper Drury, *University of Missouri–Columbia*

Doug Foyle, *Wesleyan University*

H. Richard Friman, *Marquette University*

Jean Garrison, *University of Wyoming*

Vicki Golich, *California State University–San Marcos*

Jeffrey Hart, *Indiana University*

Shareen Hertel, *University of Connecticut*

Jeanne Hey, *Miami University*

Steve Hook, *Kent State University*

Valerie Hudson, *Brigham Young University*

David Kinsella, *Portland State University*

Robert Kudrle, *University of Minnesota*

Lynn Kuzma, *University of Southern Maine*

Steve Lamy, *University of Southern California*

Jeffrey Lantis, *College of Wooster*

James McCormick, *Iowa State University*

James Mittelman, *American University*

Steven C. Poe, *University of North Texas*

Lisa Prugl, *Florida International University*

Paul Sharp, *University of Minnesota, Duluth*

David Skidmore, *Drake University*

Jennifer Sterling-Folker, *University of Connecticut*

Emek Ucarer, *Bucknell University*

Jonathan Wilkenfeld, *University of Maryland*

Titles in the Series

The Rules of the Game: A Primer on International Relations, by Mark R. Amstutz

A Tale of Two Quagmires: Iraq, Vietnam, and the Hard Lessons of War, by Kenneth J. Campbell

Celebrity Diplomacy, by Andrew F. Cooper

People Count! Networked Individuals in Global Politics, by James N. Rosenau

Paradoxes of Power: U.S. Foreign Policy in a Changing World, edited by David Skidmore

Global Democracy and the World Social Forums, by Jackie Smith et al.

Forthcoming

Development Wars: The Alter-Globalization Movement Meets Market Fundamentalism, by Robin Broad and John Cavanagh

Spirits Talking: Six Conversations on Right and Wrong in the Affairs of States, by Stephen D. Wrage